NEW DIRECTIONS FOR EVALUATION

W9-DBO-105

Sponsored by the American Evaluation Association

Editorial Policy and Procedures

New Directions for Evaluation, a quarterly sourcebook, is an official publication of the American Evaluation Association. The journal publishes empirical, methodological, and theoretical works on all aspects of evaluation. A reflective approach to evaluation is an essential strand to be woven through every issue. The editors encourage issues that have one of three foci: (1) craft issues that present approaches, methods, or techniques that can be applied in evaluation practice, such as the use of templates, case studies, or survey research; (2) professional issues that present topics of import for the field of evaluation, such as utilization of evaluation or locus of evaluation capacity; (3) societal issues that draw out the implications of intellectual, social, or cultural developments for the field of evaluation, such as the women's movement, communitarianism, or multiculturalism. A wide range of substantive domains is appropriate for *New Directions for Evaluation;* however, the domains must be of interest to a large audience within the field of evaluation. We encourage a diversity of perspectives and experiences within each issue, as well as creative bridges between evaluation and other sectors of our collective lives.

The editors do not consider or publish unsolicited single manuscripts. Each issue of the journal is devoted to a single topic, with contributions solicited, organized, reviewed, and edited by a guest editor. Issues may take any of several forms, such as a series of related chapters, a debate, or a long article followed by brief critical commentaries. In all cases, the proposals must follow a specific format, which can be obtained from the editor-in-chief. These proposals are sent to members of the editorial board and to relevant substantive experts for peer review. The process may result in acceptance, a recommendation to revise and resubmit, or rejection. However, the editors are committed to working constructively with potential guest editors to help them develop acceptable proposals.

Sandra Mathison, Editor-in-Chief
University of British Columbia
2125 Main Mall
Vancouver, BC V6T 1Z4
CANADA
e-mail: nde@eval.org

CONTENTS

Editors' Notes

We and other experienced evaluation managers have taught and consulted about managing and how difficult this work can be. Over the years, we wanted to train others in the day-to-day skills of managing studies, evaluators and other workers, and an evaluation unit, but there were few resources available, except materials for research project managers. Literature reviews, surprisingly, revealed little that was specific to managing evaluation, with volumes about general management and the manager—far too much to read, grasp, and use given that evaluation managers have little time to read and reflect.

It became quite clear, after communication with the American Evaluation Association's (AEA) Evaluation Managers and Supervisors Topical Interest Group (TIG), that managing was receiving considerably less attention in our profession than research work and that little scholarship was devoted to explicating and studying this practice. Nor has there been much attention on education in managing in and for evaluation. The active support of the TIG, especially from its leaders, Ann Maxwell and Sue Hewitt, made it fun to struggle for 2 years to get at what is managing expertise, the all-too-often-invisible, if not ineffable, work that makes for effective and efficacious evaluation practice. This issue of NDE comes out of these experiences and findings.

In the following chapters, we witness evaluation managing as a professional practice. We want to illuminate its presence, making it visible so that it can be named and seen, and then studied, taught, learned, and practiced. And evaluated. Managing evaluation covers studies, evaluators and other workers, and an evaluation unit; it includes evaluation for accountability, program improvement, and evaluation capacity building.

This issue is directed at reflecting on basic questions for our profession, the answers to which would lead us to act collectively, as a community of practice, to make managing evaluation a core professional competence. Through this discussion, we intend to give prominence to the little-noticed and too-little-regarded everyday work of managing evaluation in organizations.

Case Studies on Managing Evaluation

Four case studies are presented. Together, they provide a set of data for understanding the management, manager, and managing of evaluation studies, workers, and an evaluation unit.

NEW DIRECTIONS FOR EVALUATION, no. 121, Spring 2009 © Wiley Periodicals, Inc. and the American Evaluation Association. Published online in Wiley InterScience (www.interscience.wiley.com) • DOI: 10.1002/ev.280

The first is about the evaluation work of the Wilder Foundation research group in St. Paul, Minnesota. Wilder is a local service foundation with a research group that does internal and contract evaluation and social research, locally to internationally. The focus of this case is evaluation for program improvement. Especially clear here are the several managerial roles staff move in and out of in the research group while contracting, implementing, and using an evaluation study. The Wilder Research Center's director, Paul W. Mattessich, and two of his colleagues, Daniel P. Mueller and Cheryl A. Holm-Hansen, are the authors of an excellent practical introduction to evaluation for program managers.

The second case study, by Robert J. Rodosky and Marco A. Muñoz, is about their work for the Jefferson County (Louisville, Kentucky Public Schools. Here, an older master, Rodosky, and his younger colleague bring their perspectives to evaluation work for accountability. It is a story of how they work to create, institutionalize, sustain, and adapt to ongoing internal (school system) and external (state, federal, and community) demands for usable and timely data in the seemingly unending, ever-expanding, and speeded-up world of public education, with its locus at the confluence of law, politics, community, and education.

In the third case study, Donald W. Compton writes about his work as the first director of evaluation for the National Home Office (NHO) of the American Cancer Society (ACS). He tells how evaluation capacity building (ECB) was chosen as his strategy, and how he worked with many others within and outside ACS/NHO to build a nationwide network supporting local evaluation studies by graduate students and their faculty advisees, among others. This case shows ECB as a third managerial strategy.

The fourth case is by a highly experienced evaluation manager at the Centers for Disease Control and Prevention (CDC). Michael W. Schooley tells the story of how he came to manage, and later develop, evaluation studies, evaluators, and a heterogeneous research unit with evaluators, epidemiologists, and other researchers.

We offer a series of questions here to help focus the reading of these cases. These are intended for readers who manage evaluation, aspire to be managers of evaluation, or study the managing of evaluation.

General Questions

- Do the case studies clarify my interest in managing evaluation studies, workers, or a unit?
- How might managing expertise enhance my practice?
- How might evaluation expertise enhance my managing?

Managing Studies

- Is it useful to distinguish between what the best science for a particular study is and managing as the way to make that happen?

Managing Evaluators

- Is framing evaluators as "knowledge workers" useful in your practice?
- What do the case studies suggest about the management of evaluation staff and the managing of professional evaluators?

Managing a Unit

- What in your experience are the similarities and differences in managing a unit with a homogeneous (all evaluators) or heterogeneous (mixed group of evaluators, e.g., epidemiologist, social and behavioral scientists) group of professionals?
- How is managing an evaluation unit similar to and different from managing a restaurant, a sports team, or a small corporation?
- What is the expertise of an evaluation unit manager?
- Must evaluation unit managers be evaluators? What are the implications of this for the field, the workers, and the work?

Overall

- How do you conceive of "expertise" and skill?
- Who is the best evaluation manager you have worked for and worked with? the worst? How would you characterize their expertise and style? What ethos, expertise, and style do the best have in common? the worst? What crosses both sets?

The purpose of these questions is to orient you to reading and reflecting on the text, beginning with the case studies that follow.

Acknowledgments

We would like to thank Sandra Mathison for guiding this publication to completion. Ann Maxwell and Sue Hewitt of the American Evaluation Association's Evaluation Managers and Supervisors' TIG supported us in developing this issue and providing important feedback from the TIG membership. For their editorial contributions, we are grateful to Doris Redfield, Robert St. Pierre, Ross Vellure Roholt, Lei Zhang, William Winans, Anthony Little, and Peggy Pond. Finally, we thank the case study authors, who helped us better understand managing evaluation, from the 20th floor to the subbasement.

Donald W. Compton
Michael Baizerman
Editors

DONALD W. COMPTON *is former director of evaluation services, National Home Office, American Cancer Society, and adjunct faculty, Emory University, Rollins School of Public Health. He is the corresponding editor for this issue and reachable at donaldcompton03@comcast.net.*

MICHAEL BAIZERMAN *is professor, youth studies, School of Social Work, University of Minnesota.*

We shall not cease from exploration
And the end of all our exploring
Will be to arrive where we started
And know the place for the first time.
—T.S. Eliot, 1943

Baizerman, M., & Compton, D. W. (2009). A perspective on managing evaluation. In D. W. Compton & M. Baizerman (Eds.), *Managing program evaluation: Towards explicating a professional practice. New Directions for Evaluation, 121*, 7–15.

1

A Perspective on Managing Evaluation

Michael Baizerman, Donald W. Compton

Abstract

Managing evaluation studies, evaluators and other workers, and evaluation units is an omnipresent but almost invisible practice little studied and written about. The authors ask whether this should change and how. It is necessary to illuminate this practice before deciding, making distinctions among management, manager, and managing, the first a view from the 20th floor, the second from the 10th to fifth floors, and the last on the ground floor of everyday life. Conceptual and practical definitions drawn from practice and literature emphasize the routine, mundane nature of the work. Needed are research, analysis, and reflection on managing expertise, with a focus on the importance of expertise in evaluation research and in managing. © Wiley Periodicals, Inc.

Don Compton's dad made a building with his own hands in downtown Blacksburg, Virginia, to generate family income. For 10 years, it has been used as a restaurant, with different lessees. Only the current occupant had worked in the restaurant business before opening his place; the other lessees were a counselor and a government administrator. Each failed to make the restaurant profitable over a 3-year period. All of these professionals had "management experience," but only one was a professional "restaurant manager." Dilbert makes the issue clear (see Figure 1.1).

Figure 1.1.

Source. New York Times (2007); used with permission.

There are two distinctions here: between knowing about management and knowing managing, and applying both to a restaurant; and by contrast knowing restaurant management and restaurant managing, and using them to manage a restaurant. There is an insider-outsider distinction that it is crucial for us to grasp and reflect on as a profession: Must evaluation managers be trained, professional evaluators?

Strategy for Understanding Managing Evaluation

Managing evaluation is an almost invisible practice, one little studied and little written about. Illuminating everyday practice and perspectives on it serves to make the taken-for-granted, the seemingly invisible and often ineffable, available. In so doing, much of what is seen seems obvious, too often boring. Everyday managing is precisely about the ordinary, mundane work of managing evaluation studies, evaluators and other workers, and an evaluation unit. This is the ground of the work and it is what must be noticed, studied, taught, and learned. Once illuminated, our profession can engage findings from a recent study of job descriptions listed by the American Evaluation Association (Dewey, Montrosse, Schröter, & Sullins, 2008), where it was found that 53% sought competencies in "supervising and team management."

We came to this topic through Compton's 28 years as an evaluator and evaluation manager and Baizerman's wondering why there is such a small literature on managing evaluation. An earlier issue of *NDE* (St. Pierre, 1983) continues to be the only text on managing in general, with several other works on managing evaluation projects (Bell, 2004), managing studies (Russ-Eft & Preskill, 2001), and managing units (Chelimsky, 1994). Given the omnipresence of managing, its absence in the professional and scholarly evaluation literature is noticeable.

There are central questions for the field in the domain of managing:

- Should the evaluation field recognize managing as a core professional expertise?
- Should it promote this by legitimizing preparation of these experts and this expertise?
- What should the curriculum, pedagogy, and learning sites be?

A second set of questions gets at managing evaluation expertise:

1. What type of *evaluation* expertise is basic to managing:
   - Evaluation studies?
   - Evaluators and other workers?
   - An evaluation unit?
2. What type of *managing* expertise is basic to managing:
   - Evaluation studies?
   - Evaluator?
   - An evaluation unit?
3. What type of *evaluation* expertise is basic to managing evaluation for:
   - Accountability?
   - Program improvement?
   - Evaluation Capacity Building?
4. What type of *managing* expertise is basic to managing evaluation for:
   - Accountability?
   - Program improvement?
   - Evaluation Capacity Building?

Again, slightly different, the basic orienting questions for the profession are:

- Should evaluation as a field develop its own theory, research, practice, and evaluation approaches to managing?
- Or should we evaluate, adopt, and adapt existing management theory and practice to the evaluation field?

There are many related practical, conceptual, and theoretical issues in the practice of managing evaluation. Managing is organization work, and this is an essential of managing evaluation. Some managers are trained evaluators; many are not. What is the effect of professional background for educating and training evaluation managers? Some evaluation units are homogeneous (all trained evaluators) and some are heterogeneous. How important is this difference for training managers and in everyday managing? There are modern and postmodern evaluation strategies. Does any of this matter in training and evaluating managers? What are the skills for managing a unit in a classical Weberian formal organization in contrast to one in a rhizomic coalition or partnership of organizations (Boje, Gephart, & Thatchenkery, 1996)?

Some of the issues raised, analyzed briefly, played with, and discussed in this issue are grounded in four case studies:

1. Research and Planning Department, Wilder Research Center, Amherst H. Wilder Foundation, St. Paul, Minnesota
2. Accountability, Research and Planning Department, Jefferson County Public Schools, Louisville, Kentucky
3. Evaluation Services Department, National Home Office, American Cancer Society, Atlanta, Georgia
4. National Center for Chronic Disease Prevention and Health Promotion, Centers for Disease Control and Prevention, U.S. Department of Health and Human Services, Atlanta, Georgia

These cases get at three of the basic uses of evaluation and four of the basic types of evaluation employers. Individual authors were chosen from nominators across our profession and by their willingness to meet with us and write a case study of their work.

In addition, four interviews were conducted with evaluation unit managers. The interviewees were:

1. Diane Dunet, Centers for Disease Control and Prevention, Atlanta, Georgia
2. Wayne Stephens, Centers for Disease Control and Prevention, Atlanta
3. Robert Merritt, Centers for Disease Control and Prevention, Atlanta
4. Robert St. Pierre, STP Associates, Breckenridge, Colorado

Additionally, the case studies and interviews were chosen to understand the size and complexity of the evaluation unit as well as its organizational setting, authority, and responsibilities within the larger organization and to other stakeholders. We were aware, too, of geographic locale, professional education, work history as researchers and as managers of evaluation, and scholarly record. We also wanted to probe the managing of multiple types of evaluation studies, with multiple methodologies, budget sizes, very different time frames, and in differing (often difficult) political contexts and situations, including policy formulations, decision making, and program funding decisions.

Perspective and Bias

Our larger purpose is to enhance program evaluation's contribution to social good through more effective managing of studies, evaluators and other workers, and an evaluation unit. We want to make explicit and named, visible and analyzable, the practice of managing evaluation so it can be practiced more effectively and rightly. We tried to determine what individuals say, do, and hold to be true when they see themselves as (or working as, and are taken by others to be) managing evaluation studies, evaluators, and an evaluation shop. In this way, we want to know what managing evaluation is as expert practice and as expertise.

The case studies, interviews, and analyses are excursions (Jackson, 2007), edifications, sensitizations, and invitations to grasping and understanding managing evaluation as mundane practice. We want to focus on managing as a practical enterprise, one grounded in the everyday realities of the work, centered in a knowing, acting agent: the manager.

We had hoped to learn about managing evaluation top to bottom. Imagine an elevator that begins on the 20th floor, moves down to the 10th floor, then to the fifth floor, then to the ground floor, and finally to the

Table 1.1. Perspectives on Managing Evaluation

20th Floor	10th Floor	5th Floor	Ground Floor
Management			
Knowing what	Propositional knowledge	Applied science	Knowing how to
Knowing about science of management	Functional categories of activities (e.g., budgeting)	Knowing how to	Management roles (e.g., leader, negotiator)
		Principles of practice	Theories-in-use
		Management expertise	
		Reflected theories	
Manager			
Knowing how to	What must I do today?	Reflected theories	Theories-in-use
		Expert manager	Principles of practice
Managing			
Everyday managing as a manager	What can I do today?	Managing expertise	Self as manager
			Making sense of my managing my everyday world and my work
			"Practice wisdom," "rules of thumb," etc.
			Reflected experience of managing as a manager

Figure 1.2. The Managerial Pyramid

basement. We move from overview (20th floor) to increasingly closer views (10th and fifth floors), stopping at everyday life, the ground floor, where managing is done. Much of the management literature is at the 20th to 10th floors, with the manager literature on the 10th to fifth floors. We aspire to be firmly on the ground floor. For us, managing is the ground of the practice (Table 1.1). The managerial pyramid in Figure 1.2 shows it another way.

To better understand everyday managing, we began with the evaluation literature, and then moved outward to other academic and professional fields. The latter are voluminous and cross multiple fields. The managing evaluation literature is quite small and not reviewed fully elsewhere. We briefly present this after noting some distinctions important for our purpose. Following that, we offer conceptual and practical definitions of managing evaluation.

Management is a general field of practice, a formal organizational level, and a positional title; *manager* also is a positional social role. *Managing* is the expert activity and the expertise. *Evaluation* is the general field of practice, and *evaluation studies* is the research. The chapters in this issue of *NDE* focus on expertise in managing evaluation studies, evaluators and other workers, and an evaluation unit in recognition that this can be the expertise of trained evaluators or others holding the manager job title, or in other organizational positions or social roles.

Toward Definitions

We offer two definitions of managing evaluation, the first conceptual and the second practical. Both are tentative, an invitation for reflection and discussion, and an attempt to make visible managing expertise for analysis, empirical study, and more effective practice.

Conceptual definition. The phrase *effective managing* refers to the *everyday, mundane action* necessary in each *organizational context and moment* to make possible one or more evaluation studies, the work of evaluators, and the collective workings of an evaluation unit for the purpose of using quality evaluation for program improvement, accountability, or evaluation capacity building, among other intentions.

Effective managing means the expertise, a practical praxis of theory, concepts, and action in the service of at least an organization's mission. *Everyday, mundane* means the regular, ordinary, and (typically) taken-for-granted plane of everyday life "at work." By *action* is meant the range of typical and unusual tasks, projects, and activities necessary to make possible the work of evaluators and other workers and the evaluation unit, including the classical planning, organizing, staffing, coordinating, visioning, and so on. *Organizational context* means the social, political, cultural, and related realities of the unit, of evaluation as such, and of each evaluation study within the larger organization, in the program/project/organization being evaluated, and in related and relevant organizational networks. *Moment* is the emergent, present, and succeeding "nows"—future, present, and past—as they are implicated in the flow of work of managing studies, workers, and an evaluation unit.

Practical definition. The phrase *effective managing of evaluation* means the practical, everyday, professional expertise necessary to bring about the implementation and use of quality studies, the development of productive workers, and the sustaining of a well-run, ongoing, and influential evaluation unit.

These definitions and earlier questions can be used to reflect on an actual job description for managing evaluation.

Position Guide: Director of Outcomes and Evaluation

> The Director of Outcomes and Evaluation is responsible for implementing an outcomes management system, directing evaluations for existing and newly funded projects, and providing technical assistance to support systems of care throughout the project. The Director seeks out the latest national information, reviews data collected, and through analysis, provides the project with usable information for program and outcome improvement. Will be part of the Management Team, meeting as needed.

Minimum Qualifications:

- *Masters required, PhD. Preferred—in psychology, sociology, public health or other human service*
- *Minimum of three years experience conducting program evaluation and managing outcomes for community-based programs*
- *Expertise in strength-based, crisis intervention, systems theory; multisystems care coordination and case management*

NEW DIRECTIONS FOR EVALUATION • DOI: 10.1002/ev

- Strong knowledge of and genuine respect for youth and adults with mental health issues and a firm commitment to empowering their families
- Demonstrated competence in evaluating services and resources for culturally diverse populations

Managerial/community relations experience should include:

- Supervisory experience that promotes leadership and initiative in line staff, successful team building, consensus building, conflict resolution, staff development and advocacy
- Knowledge of training and evaluating staff
- Developing and maintaining positive working relationships with private and public providers, funding bodies, families, consumer advocacy groups
- Presenting outcomes and explaining methodology to outside groups
- Budget management

Responsibilities:

The Director of Outcomes and Evaluation has specific responsibility for:

Outcomes and Evaluation

a. Developing outcomes that are project-specific, research-based, and useful to project stakeholders
b. Identifying measurement techniques and data collection procedures that are reliable, valid, and appropriate for the populations being served
c. Training project staff in data collection, survey administration, and data entry protocols, including data entry into The Clinical Manager (TCM)
d. Designing and conduction project evaluations for existing and newly funded projects and reporting findings to project stakeholders, funding agencies, and the community
e. Maintaining an updated knowledge base of best practices research to inform project improvements, develop effective outcome measures, and design appropriate evaluations
f. Providing training and assistance to project staff and stakeholders in the effective use and interpretation of evaluation results and outcomes data
g. Tracking local, state, and national social indicators to identify service delivery gaps and monitor trends
h. Providing technical assistance to develop and support systems of care and evidence based practice
i. Disseminating project findings to local, state, and national audiences
j. Supervising all evaluation and data collection activities and implementing protocols to insure quality assurance and the protection of human subjects

Minimum Requirements

1. *Ability to effectively manage multiple priorities simultaneously*
2. *Ability to provide outstanding service to all individuals inside and outside the organization*
3. *Ability to effectively communicate to various internal and external audiences both in person and through various electronic media*
4. *Ability to use and a working knowledge of personal computers and Microsoft Office products (Windows, Word, Excel, PowerPoint, Project, Visio, Outlook, and Explorer)*
5. *Knowledge of statistical software including SPSS*
6. *Ability to use The Clinical Manager software package*
7. *Hold a valid drivers license and car insurance*

References

Bell, J. B. (2004). Managing evaluation projects. In J. S.Wholey, H. P. Hatry, & K. Newcomer (Eds.), *Handbook of practical program evaluation* (2nd ed., pp. 571–603). San Francisco: Jossey-Bass.

Boje, D. M., Gephart, R. P., & Thatchenkery, T. J. (Eds.). (1996). *Postmodern management and organization theory.* Thousand Oaks, CA: Sage.

Chelimsky, E. (1994). Making evaluation units effective. In J. S. Wholey, H. P. Hatry, & K. Newcomer (Eds.), *Handbook of practical program evaluation* (pp. 493–509). San Francisco: Jossey-Bass.

Dewey, J. D., Montrosse, B. E., Schröter, D.C., & Sullins, C. D. (2008). Evaluator competencies: What's taught versus what's sought. *American Journal of Evaluation, 19*(3), 268–287.

Dilbert. (2007, November 11). *New York Times,* p. BU10.

Jackson, M. (2007). *Excursions.* Durham, NC: Duke University Press.

Russ-Eft, D. F., & Preskill, H. S. (2001). *Evaluation in organizations: A systematic approach to enhancing learning, performance, and change.* Cambridge, MA: Perseus.

St. Pierre, R. (Ed.). (1983). Management and organization of program evaluation. *New Directions for Evaluation, 18,* 1–126.

MICHAEL BAIZERMAN is *professor, youth studies, School of Social Work, University of Minnesota.*

DONALD W. COMPTON is *former director of evaluation services, National Home Office, American Cancer Society; and adjunct faculty, Emory University, Rollins School of Public Health. He is the corresponding editor for this issue and is reachable at donaldcompton03@comcast.net.*

Compton, D. W. (2009). Where is the literature in evaluation on managing studies, evaluators, and evaluation units? In D. W. Compton & M. Baizerman (Eds.), *Managing program evaluation: Towards explicating a professional practice. New Directions for Evaluation, 121*, 17–25.

2

Where Is the Literature in Evaluation on Managing Studies, Evaluators, and Evaluation Units?

Donald W. Compton

Abstract

On the basis of a multistage exploration of evaluation texts, electronic searches, and nominations from the field and from managing social science, the author concludes there is little research literature on managing evaluation studies, evaluators and other workers, and evaluation units. The discussion explores what this limited literature tells us about managing evaluation. Although these findings are consistent with an earlier literature review (St. Pierre, 1983), here the reasons for the paucity are explored. © Wiley Periodicals, Inc.

To begin this review of literature in evaluation on managing, we return to the *New Directions for Program Evaluation* issue on the organization and management of program evaluation (St. Pierre, 1983, p. 1):

A review of the literature in this area (St. Pierre, 1982) reveals very few articles. The major evaluation journals and handbooks have ignored the topic. Further, the subject is covered lightly, if at all, in most evaluation texts; it is not a common subject in graduate training; and, according to Anderson and

Ball (1978, p. 169), forty-four "people whose opinions we would value and which would seem to carry weight in the field" did not perceive it to be a particularly important topic for graduate training in evaluation research. Of thirty-two evaluation-related skills and content areas, these forty-four experts rated only two–job analysis and case study methodology–as less essential than management skills.

Twenty-six years later, our review found that little has changed. Although there is an enormous amount of literature on management and managing in general and specific to many fields, such as nursing (Sullivan & Decker, 2009), hospitals (Grinspun, 2000), education (Bush & Bell, 2002), higher education (Higgerson & Rehwaldt, 1993), human resource (Byars & Rue, 2004), and of course business (Caroselli & Formisano, 2000), there is very little recent evaluation literature on these topics.

Method

A four-stage strategy was used to find and assess a literature for review.

Stage one: We looked through standard evaluation books and electronic databases for the key terms *management of evaluation, managing evaluation,* and *evaluation manager.* Nominations for relevant literature were also sought from the American Evaluation Association's Evaluation Managers and Supervisors Topical Interest Group (TIG). Every item found was read and categorized as the managing of evaluation studies, workers, or units.

Stage two: Using analogy, we then followed the same procedure in the field of managing social research. Only one book was found, and it is cited in the references for this chapter (Tarling, 2006).

Stage three: After reading items in stages one and two, we followed leads to managing in other fields, such as nursing and education, which have a far more developed literature on managing. For example, an Internet search using the term *educational management* produced 31 million results.

Stage four: Both editors read in the related areas of management science, the role of the manager, organizational development, and similar topics so as to enrich perspectives and context.

In the discussion here, we focus primarily on the literature from within the field of evaluation. Unlike Wren (2005), we do not trace the evolution of management theory; unlike Birnbaum (2000), we do not examine management fads, and we did not search other fields for literature that could be adapted. We stayed in our own back yard. It is precisely the absence of literature that led us to working on this volume. St. Pierre said that this was his motive, too. See Table 2.1 for a summary of literature included in this review. The left column of Table 2.1 summarizes literature cited in this review and select literature reviewed for this volume is included in the right column. It shows that there is almost no literature related to managing

Table 2.1. Foci in the Managing Evaluation Literature

Literature Cited in Literature Review	Select Literature Reviewed	
Managing Studies	American Management Association (2008) www.amanet.org	Mathison, S. (2005)
Bell, J. B. (2004)	Anderson, S. B., & Ball, S. (1978)	Mattessich, P. (2003)
Centers for Disease Control and Prevention (2008)	Aspinwall, K. (1992)	McDermott, R. J., & Sarvela, P. D. (1999)
Development Assistance Committee (2006)	Bamberger, M., Rugh, J., & Mabry, L. (2006)	McGee, J. (2006)
Lunt, N., Davidson, C., & McKegg, K. (2003)	Benner, P., Tanner, C., & Chesla, C. (1996)	Moynihan, D. P. (2008)
Owen, J. M. (2007)	Birnbaum, R. (2000)	Patton, M. Q. (1980)
Russ-Eft, D. F., & Preskill, H. S. (2001)	Bush, T. (1989)	Patton, M. Q. (1981)
Stevahn, L., King, J.A., Ghere, G.A., & Minnema, J. (2005)	Bush, T., & Bell, L. (2002)	Patton, M. Q. (1982)
Stufflebeam, D. L., & Shinkfield, A. J. (2007)	Byars, L. L., & Rue, L. W. (2004)	Patton, M. Q. (2008)
Western Michigan University (2008)	Caroselli, M., & Formisano, R. A. (2000)	Pawson, R., & Tilley, N. (1997)
	Chelimsky, E., & Shadish, W. R. (1997)	Posavac, E. J., & Carey, R. G. (2003)
	Chen, H. T. (1990)	Preskill, H. S., & Torres, R. T. (1999)
	Collins, H. M., & Evans, R. (2007)	Rist, R., & Stame, N. (2006)
Managing Staff	Davenport, T. H., & Prusak, L. (2000)	Rossi, P. H., & Freeman, H. E. (1999)
	Davenport, T. H. (2005)	Rue, L. W., & Byars, L. L. (1977)
Davenport, T. H. (2005)	Dessinger, J. C., & Moseley, J. L. (2004)	Schalock, R. L. (2001)
	Donaldson, S. I., & Scriven, M. (2003)	Sonnichsen, R. C. (2000)
Managing Units	Drucker, P. F. (2001)	Squires, G. (2001)
	Fetterman, D. M., Kaftarian, S. J., & Wandersman, A. (1995)	Stake, R. (1998)
Chelimsky, E. (1994)	Goldsmith, A. A. (1995)	Stuckenbruck, L. C. (1981)
Lunt, N., Davidson, C., & McKegg, K. (2003)	Gray, S. T. (1998)	Suchman, E. A. (1967)
St. Pierre, R. G. (1982)	Grinspun, D. (2000)	Sullivan, E. J., & Decker, P. J. (2009)
Shadish, W. R., Cook, T. D., & Leviton, L. C. (1991)	Hamel, G. (2007)	Tarling, R. (2006)
Wholey, J. S., Hatry, H. P., & Newcomer, K. E. (2004)	Herman, J. L., Morris, L. L., & Fitz-Gibbon, T. (1987)	Weiss, C. H. (1972)
	Kushner, S. (2000)	Weiss, C. H., & Weiss, C. H. (1998)
	Legge, K. (1995)	Wren, D. A. (2005)
	Love, A. J. (1991)	

evaluators or an evaluation unit. However, some literature was found on managing one study or multiple studies. Discussions of managing studies did not typically focus on the purpose of the studies, politics surrounding them, or other contextual factors.

What Does the Literature Teach Us About Managing Evaluation Studies, Staff, and Units?

The focus of this book is on the managing of evaluation studies, workers, and units, and each of these is addressed separately, even though in practice they are not so distinct and surely not mutually exclusive. Within evaluation, there is literature on the management of studies, but little on managing workers or units.

Managing Studies. The evaluation literature includes several books with sections or chapters on managing evaluation studies (Bell, 2004; Centers for Disease Control and Prevention, 2008; Development Assistance Committee, 2006; Lunt, Davidson, & McKegg, 2003; Owen, 2007; Russ-Eft & Preskill, 2001; Stufflebeam & Shinkfield, 2007).

The project management literature includes a significant number of texts and other resources adaptable for managing evaluation studies (Stuckenbruck, 1981). A few examples show their orientation.

Bell (2004, p. 571) defines evaluation project management as "a process of considerations, decisions, and activities engaged in by the leadership of an evaluation project to facilitate its conduct." He notes that it is more art than science and provides practical suggestions for evaluation project management within the categories of developing rational proposals, clarifying the evaluation mandate, staffing and organizing for results, making assignments productive, monitoring interim progress, and ensuring product quality and usefulness (p. 602). He notes that "a valid and useful evaluation depends as much on effective management as [on] an elegant evaluation design" (p. 603).

In a similar sense, Russ-Eft and Preskill discuss the importance of managing evaluation by developing various management plans that "can help ensure that the evaluation is implemented as planned, that people responsible for various tasks do indeed carry out their responsibilities, and that any potential obstacles can be considered ahead of time" (2001, p. 383). They offer examples along with a sample evaluation budget, and they describe the tasks of managing the evaluation:

* Monitoring the evaluation project's tasks and personnel
* Staying on schedule or negotiating schedule changes
* Monitoring the evaluation budget
* Staying on budget or negotiating changes
* Keeping the client and stakeholders informed of progress and any problems that occur

NEW DIRECTIONS FOR EVALUATION • DOI: 10.1002/ev

A more specific strategy comes from Western Michigan University's Evaluation Checklists Project (www.wmich.edu/evalctr/checklists/), which includes tools for guiding and judging evaluations. Among the checklists most useful for managing evaluation are the Evaluation Contracts Checklist and the Evaluation Plans and Operations Checklist (Stufflebeam), the Utilization-Focused Evaluation (U-FE Checklist; Patton), the Checklist for Negotiating an Agreement to Evaluate an Educational Programme (Stake), and the Budget Development Checklist (Horn).

In a different vein and in a substantive and typical discussion, Lunt, Davidson, and McKegg (2003) devote one chapter of their reader to managing evaluation, with a focus on determining the scope of the project, internal versus external capacity to conduct a study, development of a study proposal, the selection criteria for a contractor, the contract, and ongoing contract management. Four case studies are presented, with the overarching theme that effective partnerships are the key to good contracting and evaluation.

The Development Assistance Committee (2006) produced Guidance for Managing Joint Evaluations as a practical guide for managers of joint evaluations of development assistance programs, and this seems especially useful in that context. It describes the most common management structure for large joint evaluations as a "two-tier management system consisting of (a) a broad membership steering committee and (b) a smaller management group that runs the day-to-day business of the evaluation" (p. 20). Clearly, this approach can be adapted for use in other contexts.

Insiders (evaluators) or outsiders (management professionals with little or no professional training in evaluation) and other professionals working as managers manage studies. Who manages these managers? Who manages evaluators *as* evaluators?

Managing Staff. Even though there is a huge amount of general literature on managing and supervision, no literature was found specifically about managing evaluators. One relevant resource is *Thinking for a Living*, which is about "knowledge workers": those with "high degrees of expertise, education, or experience, and [for whom] the primary purpose of their jobs involves the creation, distribution, or application of knowledge" (Davenport, 2005, p. 10). A final chapter is devoted to contrasting traditional management approaches to those most effective with knowledge workers.

Of particular importance is the notion that "managers of knowledge workers have to be knowledge workers themselves; they are 'player/coaches.'"

Evaluators may work in homogeneous (evaluators only) or heterogeneous (evaluators and other researchers) groups or in other organizational units. Managing professional staff and managing studies comes together in many evaluation units.

NEW DIRECTIONS FOR EVALUATION • DOI: 10.1002/ev

Managing Units. A small amount of literature was found on managing evaluation units. However, in their chapter on Joe Wholey's approach to evaluation, Shadish, Cook, and Leviton (1991, p. 245) note that "in organizing and managing evaluation, the first task is to work with high-level managers and policymakers to establish policy—how evaluation resources are to be used, what types of evaluation activities are to be given high priority, and what results are expected from evaluation" (Wholey, 1983, p. 168). Then resources are mobilized, evaluation staff and contractors are hired, and the evaluation office is integrated with the program.

Two papers by St. Pierre (1982) and Chelimsky (1994) discuss aspects of managing an in-house evaluation team or unit in the federal government. St. Pierre's focus is on planning for procurements, issues related to doing the work in-house as opposed to contracting it out, and considerations for managing the contractor/practitioner team, among others. In citing Lewis (1980), he notes that, "Unfortunately good evaluators are not always competent managers and so a conflict of interest can exist—to advance in the field you must manage evaluations: large studies require both managerial and technical expertise; and while most clients want project directors to have excellent technical skills, many excellent evaluators are poor managers" (St. Pierre, 1982, p. 100).

Chelimsky addresses managing evaluation units from the perspective of making them effective in organizational contexts and establishing the legitimacy of the unit within the organization. She describes how

> it is important to understand the political environments of both the unit's main customer and the larger organization in which it is embedded. The requirements generated by both these analyses are the best bases for determining the characteristics of the evaluation unit that will allow it to survive and succeed. Maintaining the confidence of top management, recruiting high-quality staff, selecting the "right" topics to evaluate, and producing strong studies are also important aspects of planning. (Chelimsky, 1994, p. 507)

She presents guidelines for working with "customers" adopted by the General Accounting Office, including negotiating the issues to evaluate in terms of the information need, holding frequent briefings and maintaining continuing communications, developing a mix of evaluation tools, and obtaining feedback.

Finally, the competency framework for evaluation by Stevahn, King, Ghere, and Minnema (2005) includes project management, staff supervision, budgeting for evaluation, and other related knowledge and skills.

Conclusions

There is limited literature on the managing of studies, while the managing of workers and units is largely unwritten. From these findings, we find it reasonable to ask:

- Why is there such a paucity of work on management and managing within the evaluation field?
- Do managers of evaluation conceive of themselves as "managers"?
- What literature do managers use to understand and enhance their practice?
- What does this paucity of indigenous literature tell us after 40 years of practice—doing evaluation research, being evaluators, and working in evaluation units?

This limited literature stands in contrast to the seemingly boundless and accelerating work on management and managing in other fields and in general. This makes the contrast especially stark. Could it be that the very absence of a literature on managing in evaluation tells us that its practitioners do not write about this aspect of their practice, that scholars do not focus here, or that the broader management literature is read and adapted? Can it be that we in evaluation who manage do not see ourselves as managers, or see what we do as management or managing?

We need an appreciation of how managing as mundane, everyday work might be invisible. Clearly, empirical research is needed.

References

American Management Association. (2008). Retrieved July 21, 2008, from http://www.amanet.org

Anderson, S. B., & Ball, S. (1978). *The profession and practice of program evaluation* (1st ed.). San Francisco: Jossey-Bass.

Aspinwall, K. (1992). *Managing evaluation in education: A developmental approach.* London: Routledge.

Bamberger, M., Rugh, J., & Mabry, L. (2006). *RealWorld evaluation: Working under budget, time, data, and political constraints.* Thousand Oaks, CA: Sage.

Bell, J. B. (2004). Managing evaluation projects. In J. S. Wholey, H. P. Hatry, & K. E. Newcomer (Eds.), *Handbook of practical program evaluation* (2nd ed., pp. 571–603). San Francisco: Jossey-Bass.

Benner, P., Tanner, C., & Chesla, C. (1996). *Expertise in nursing practice.* New York: Springer.

Birnbaum, R. (2000). *Management fads in higher education: Where they come from, what they do, why they fail.* San Francisco: Jossey-Bass.

Bush, T. (1989). *Managing education theory and practice.* Milton Keynes, England: Open University Press.

Bush, T., & Bell, L. (2002). *The principles and practice of educational management: Principles and practice.* London: Paul Chapman.

Byars, L. L., & Rue, L. W. (2004). *Human resource management* (7th ed.). Boston: McGraw-Hill/Irwin.

Caroselli, M., & Formisano, R. A. (2000). *Leadership skills for managers.* New York: McGraw-Hill.

Centers for Disease Control and Prevention (2008). *Introduction to process evaluation in tobacco use prevention and control.* Atlanta, GA: U.S. Department of Health and Human Services, Centers for Disease Control and Prevention, National Center for Chronic Disease Prevention and Health Promotion, Office on Smoking and Health.

Chelimsky, E. (1994). Making evaluation units effective. In J. S. Wholey, H. P. Hatry, & K. E. Newcomer (Eds.), *Handbook of practical program evaluation* (pp. 493–509). San Francisco: Jossey-Bass.

Chelimsky, E., & Shadish, W. R. (1997). *Evaluation for the 21st century: A handbook.* Thousand Oaks, CA: Sage.

Chen, H. T. (1990). *Theory-driven evaluations.* Thousand Oaks, CA: Sage.

Collins, H. M., & Evans, R. (2007). *Rethinking expertise.* Chicago: University of Chicago Press.

Davenport, T. H. (2005). *Thinking for a living: How to get better performance and results from knowledge workers.* Boston: Harvard Business School Press.

Davenport, T. H., & Prusak, L., (2000). *Working knowledge: How organizations manage what they know.* Boston: Harvard Business School Press.

Dessinger, J. C., & Moseley, J. L. (2004). *Confirmative evaluation: Practical strategies for valuing continuous improvement.* San Francisco: Pfeiffer.

Development Assistance Committee. (2006). *Guidance for managing joint evaluations.* Retrieved September 10, 2008, from http:www.oecd.org/dac/evaluation

Donaldson, S. I., & Scriven, M. (2003). *Evaluating social programs and problems: Visions for the new millennium.* Mahwah, NJ: Erlbaum.

Drucker, P. F. (2001). *The essential Drucker: Selections from the management works of Peter F. Drucker* (1st ed.). New York: Harper Business.

Fetterman, D. M., Kaftarian, S. J., & Wandersman, A. (1995). *Empowerment evaluation knowledge and tools for self-assessment & accountability.* Thousand Oaks, CA: Sage.

Goldsmith, A. A. (1995). Making managers more effective: Applications of strategic management. Working paper, USAID's Implementing Policy Change Project.

Gray, S. T. (1998). *Evaluation with power: A new approach to organizational effectiveness, empowerment, and excellence.* San Francisco: Jossey-Bass.

Grinspun, D. (2000). Taking care of the bottom line: Shifting paradigms in hospital management. In D. L. Gustafson (Ed.), *Care and consequences: Health care reform and its impact on Canadian women.* Halifax: Fernwood.

Hamel, G. (2007). *The future of management.* Boston: Harvard Business School Press.

Herman, J. L., Morris, L. L., & Fitz-Gibbon, C. T. (1987). *Evaluator's handbook* (1st ed.). Thousand Oaks, CA: Sage.

Higgerson, M. L., & Rehwaldt, S. S. (1993). *Complexities of higher education administration.* Boston: Anker.

Kushner, S. (2000). *Personalizing evaluation.* London: Sage.

Legge, K. (1995). *Human resource management: Rhetorics and realities.* Basingstoke, England: MacMillan Business.

Lewis, J. H. (1980). Training evaluators of social experiments and programs. In L. Sechrest (Ed.), *New Directions for Program Evaluation, 8,* 39–48.

Love, A. J. (1991). *Internal evaluation building organizations from within.* Thousand Oaks: Sage.

Lunt, N., Davidson, C., & McKegg, K. (2003). *Evaluating policy and practice: A New Zealand reader.* Auckland: Pearson Prentice Hall.

Mathison, S. (Ed.) (2005). *Encyclopedia of evaluation.* Thousand Oaks, CA: Sage.

Mattessich, P. (2003). *The manager's guide to program evaluation: Planning, contracting, and managing for useful results.* St. Paul, MN: Wilder Research Center.

McDermott, R. J., & Sarvela, P. D. (1999). *Health education evaluation and measurement: A practitioner's perspective* (2nd ed.). Hightstown, NJ: WCB/McGraw-Hill.

McGee, J. (2006). Strategic Management. In C. Cooper, C. Argyris, & W. Starbuck (Eds.), *Blackwell encyclopedia of management* (2nd ed.). Malden, MA: Wiley-Blackwell.

Moynihan, D. P. (2008). *The dynamics of performance evaluation.* Washington, DC: Georgetown University Press.

Owen, J. M. (2007). *Program evaluation forms and approaches* (3rd ed.). New York: Guilford Press.

Patton, M. Q. (1980). *Qualitative evaluation methods.* Thousand Oaks, CA: Sage.

Patton, M. Q. (1981). *Creative evaluation.* Thousand Oaks, CA: Sage.

Patton, M. Q. (1982). *Practical evaluation.* Thousand Oaks, CA: Sage.

Patton, M. Q. (2008). *Utilization-focused evaluation*. Thousand Oaks, CA: Sage.

Pawson, R., & Tilley, N. (1997). *Realistic evaluation*. London: Sage.

Posavac, E. J., & Carey, R. G. (2003). *Program evaluation methods and case studies* (6th ed.). Upper Saddle River, NJ: Prentice Hall.

Preskill, H. S., & Torres, R. T. (1999). *Evaluative inquiry for learning in organizations*. Thousand Oaks, CA: Sage.

Rist, R., & Stame, N. (Eds.) (2006). From studies to streams: Managing evaluative systems. *Comparative Policy Evaluation, 12.* New Brunswick, NJ: Transaction.

Rossi, P. H., & Freeman, H. E. (1999). *Evaluation: A systematic approach* (6th ed.). Thousand Oaks, CA: Sage.

Rue, L. W., & Byars, L. L. (1977). *Management theory and application*. Homewood, IL: R. D. Irwin.

Russ-Eft, D. F., & Preskill, H. S. (2001). *Evaluation in organizations: A systematic approach to enhancing learning, performance, and change*. Cambridge, MA: Perseus.

Schalock, R. L. (2001). *Outcome-based evaluation* (2nd ed.). New York: Kluwer Academic/Plenum.

Shadish, W. R., Cook, T. D., & Leviton, L. C. (1991). *Foundations of program evaluation theories of practice*. Thousand Oaks, CA: Sage.

Sonnichsen, R. C. (2000). *High impact internal evaluation: A practitioner's guide to evaluating and consulting inside organizations*. Thousand Oaks, CA: Sage.

Squires, G. (2001). Management as a professional discipline. *Journal of Management Studies, 38,* 473–487.

St. Pierre, R. G. (1982). Management of federally funded evaluation research: Building evaluation teams. *Evaluation Review, 6,* 94–113.

St. Pierre, R. G. (1983). Management and organization of program evaluation. *New Directions for Program Evaluation, 18*(June), 1–3.

Stevahn, L., King J., Ghere, G., & Minnema, J. (2005). Establishing essential competencies for program evaluators. *American Journal of Evaluation, 26,* 43–59.

Stuckenbruck, L. C. (1981). *The implementation of project management: The professional's handbook*. Drexel Hill, PA: Project Management Institute.

Stufflebeam, D. L., & Shinkfield, A. J. (2007). *Evaluation theory, models, and applications* (1st ed.). San Francisco: Jossey-Bass.

Suchman, E. A. (1967). *Evaluative research: Principles and practice in public service and social action programs*. New York: Russell Sage Foundation.

Sullivan, E. J., & Decker, P. J. (2009). *Effective leadership and management in nursing* (5th ed.) Upper Saddle River, NJ: Prentice Hall.

Tarling, R. (2006). *Managing social research: A practical guide*. London: Routledge.

Weiss, C. H. (1972). *Evaluation research: Methods for assessing program effectiveness*. Englewood Cliffs, NJ: Prentice-Hall.

Weiss, C. H., & Weiss, C. H. (1998). *Evaluation methods for studying programs and policies* (2nd ed.) Upper Saddle River, NJ: Prentice Hall.

Western Michigan University. (2008). *Evaluation checklists project*. Retrieved June 3, 2008, from http://www.wmich.edu/evalctr/checklists

Wholey, J. S. (1983). *Evaluation and effective public management*. Boston: Little, Brown.

Wholey, J. S., Hatry, H. P., & Newcomer, K. E. (2004). *Handbook of practical program evaluation* (2nd ed.). San Francisco: Jossey-Bass.

Wren, D. A. (2005). *The evolution of management thought* (4th ed.). New York: Wiley.

DONALD W. COMPTON is former director of evaluation services, National Home Office, American Cancer Society; and adjunct faculty, Emory University, Rollins School of Public Health. He is the corresponding editor for this issue and is reachable at donaldcompton03@comcast.net.

Mattessich, P. W., Mueller, D. P., & Holm-Hansen, C. A. (2009). Managing evaluation for program improvement at the Wilder Foundation. In D. W. Compton & M. Baizerman (Eds.), *Managing program evaluation: Towards explicating a professional practice. New Directions for Evaluation, 121,* 27–42.

3

Managing Evaluation for Program Improvement at the Wilder Foundation

Paul W. Mattessich, Daniel P. Mueller,
Cheryl A. Holm-Hansen

Abstract

The authors tell about their heterogeneous 91 person research and evaluation unit at an operating foundation in St. Paul, Minnesota. They focus on evaluation for program improvement, one of several purposes of studies they work on. The three authors write from their different manager positions within the unit. Included are the context of the organization, strategic principles of their work and how it fits into a program improvement model. Mattessich writes as the executive director and details his day-to-day evaluation work. Mueller writes as the associate director, who oversees most of the unit's evaluation work, while Holm-Hansen writes as a consulting scientist who leads a core research team of four to six. © Wiley Periodicals, Inc.

Building evaluation capacity and conducting ongoing evaluation of multiple programs within a single organization, in order to contribute continuously to program improvement—how can this occur? This chapter outlines how we have built evaluation capacity and developed an internal program evaluation system for the Wilder Foundation's human services programs.

Stockdill, Baizerman, and Compton define evaluation capacity building as "intentional work to continuously create and sustain overall organizational processes that make quality evaluation and its uses routine" (2002, p. 14). Their paper also says that evaluation capacity building activities work to create and sustain spaces for professional expert program evaluation and its uses. The description of our work illustrates how such a space can be created.

Managing Evaluation at the Wilder Foundation: Context

The Amherst H. Wilder Foundation, a public charity established in 1906, has the mission "to promote the general welfare of persons resident or located in the greater Saint Paul metropolitan area by all appropriate means." The foundation contributes endowment earnings to operate programs (rather than making grants to other organizations). Client services involve more than 600 staff in some 50 programs, focusing primarily on five areas:

- School success programs to improve the educational achievement of underachieving urban students
- Troubled-children and families programs, such as mental health care and residential care for children with serious problems functioning in their homes, schools, and other community settings
- Affordable housing for low-income and older people
- Community-based services for low-income aging persons
- Public leadership and demonstration to improve the quality of life and the quality of services in the region

The foundation serves more than 10,000 people a year, from diverse racial groups; the foundation's direct services target the eastern portion of Minnesota's Twin Cities region (ranked 16th among the 25 most populous U.S. urban regions). In recent years, Saint Paul has become racially and culturally very diversified, requiring new approaches to service delivery; the median age of the population has increased, intensifying issues related to the elderly.

Wilder Research. Beyond direct services, the foundation commits itself to research. The Wilder Research mission is to "improve the lives of individuals, families, and communities through human services research." Wilder's first study was a study of housing and sanitation and led to the development of housing ordinances throughout the United States (Aronovici, 1917).

Currently, Wilder Research does program evaluation, conducts studies of community trends, and synthesizes information about effective services into reports that support program design, funding, and policy making. We issue publications ranging from one-page fact sheets to books. Our primary audience consists of managers of nonprofit and government programs, policy makers, funders, and others who shape human service, education, public health, and community development programs. Twenty percent of our work occurs for the Wilder Foundation, 80 percent for other organizations or for the community at large.

We have a staff of 91:

- Research—about 30, most with a graduate degree and experience in various social sciences. They design and oversee studies, with responsibilities commensurate with their level of expertise.
- Core units—about 30, who perform the core support functions described later in this chapter.
- On call survey—about 30, who conduct interviews or perform research assistant tasks.

Figure 3.1 depicts our organizational structure.

Research units, consisting of two to 11 staff, appear around the outside of the "donut." Each unit manages its own work, developing annual plans, establishing budgets, and developing strategies for contributing to the mission of Wilder Research.

Core units consist of Data Collection (staff for survey interviewing, focus groups, and other activities to collect, compile, and organize information); Data Analysis (information technology specialists and statisticians); Administrative Support (staff for document production,

Figure 3.1. Organizational Structure of Wilder Research

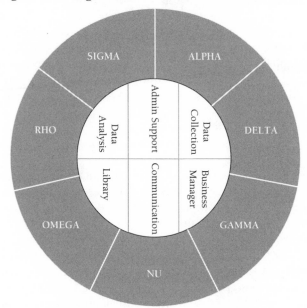

word processing, and office infrastructure); Library/Knowledge Management (staff who maintain the library, do literature searches, and supply other information support); Communications (staff for editing, writing, media relations, and conference planning); and Finance (business manager to manage financial operations).

For every project, research unit staff collaborate with core unit managers to co-design studies and assign core unit staff. Research units do internal work (for foundation programs) and external work (for other organizations). Most internal work consists of program evaluation; some involves needs assessment, strategic planning, and literature reviews to inform practice.

Strategic Principles Underlying Our Work. Several principles underlie our structure, staffing, and approach. They constitute core elements of our strategy for nurturing a strong research organization, and for effective internal evaluation capacity building for program improvement and other purposes.

We value a multidisciplinary staff, representing many social sciences. We feel that multiple disciplines enhance our ability to bring useful research into diverse and complex environments. Cross-disciplinary collaboration, in the design of both our general approach to evaluation and specific projects, sharpens our focus. It stimulates creativity.

Second, researchers work as generalists. We expect them to pursue multiple topic areas. Nonetheless, staff typically become more skilled in research related to certain topics or types of programs. Over time, they tend to specialize in those areas and less in others.

Third, we dedicate all our efforts to the missions of the Wilder Foundation and Wilder Research. This gives staff a sense of direction within which they pursue the missions in whatever way works best for them.

Fourth, we expect "entrepreneurism" among our researchers, especially unit managers. Research managers work within operating and financial guidelines established for Wilder Research as a whole. They pursue new projects and respond to requests for work from programs inside and outside the foundation. Research managers establish budgets for their units; they hire and recruit their own staff.

Fifth, we employ multiple methods in evaluation. We do not subscribe to one view of research design; we do not feel that any single method serves all circumstances.

Sixth, we establish quality standards for program evaluation. These include interviewing standards from the American Association of Public Opinion Research, and minimum sample sizes and table sizes necessary for reporting data. The standards include "style" requirements, such as the requirement that factual rendition of key data must be separate from interpretation of findings. (Values should not influence presentation of facts; values can, and should influence interpretation of facts.)

Seventh, we are nonpartisan. If a potential audience might suspect a political intent in a study, we typically establish an advisory committee to

Figure 3.2. Program Evaluation as Part of an Ongoing Cycle

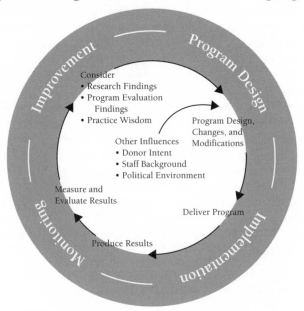

represent several points of view and offer advice on methods that will produce findings acceptable to audiences with varying political perspectives.

Eighth, we view evaluation as part of an ongoing process of program improvement that informs service providers. See Figure 3.2 (from Mattessich, 2003).

These principles fit optimally with our environment, which consists of multifarious programs serving varied people through multiple services, different philosophies about the best ways to do program evaluation, and program managers with diverse levels of readiness for, and acceptance of, research and evaluation.

Evaluation at the Wilder Foundation. From 1940 to 1970, Wilder Research used evaluation methodologies that offered systematic description and counting of inputs, activities, and outputs. Outcomes were occasionally measured but were more often assumed, given that programs produced their intended outputs. In 1976, the foundation's board of directors passed a resolution to require evaluation in all foundation programs. It strengthened and expanded Wilder Research to conduct internal program evaluation and do other forms of research and consulting, mostly local but also national and international. In the late 1970s, research staff modeled evaluation upon then-current approaches to mental health services evaluation (Davidoff, Guttentag, & Offutt, 1977). The foundation computerized a client record system that recorded client demographics, services received, and one or more "problems" for each client. Evaluation consisted of monitoring diagnosed problems over time, from intake to termination and beyond, to determine if the service resolved clients' problems.

Evaluation evolved to include measurement of both outcomes (not necessarily client "problems") and client satisfaction. Evaluation designs were customized, as much as possible, for specific programs or for clusters of related programs. Unique outcomes were measured. However, use of standardized assessment forms (such as the Achenbach Child Behavior Checklist for children's programs, activities of daily living scales for older clients) became favored because such tools enabled programs to adopt measures of optimal functioning with established validity and reliability, and to compare themselves to baselines.

Evaluation designs often involved follow-up of clients after program completion. Wilder Research interviewers called clients (or parents for minors) to gather information, sometimes using standardized checklists as mentioned above.

During the 1990s, as described later in this chapter, the nature of evaluation activities changed, primarily for financial reasons.

The Executive Director Perspective

We represent three roles in the processes of evaluation capacity building and implementation of program evaluation. As Wilder Research executive director, I (coauthor Mattessich) pay attention to how our internal program evaluation fits within our complete range of work and within the range of organizations we serve. I also look holistically at the quality of staff's work. Dan Mueller, as Wilder Research Center associate director, supervises senior research staff conducting internal program evaluation; he serves as liaison with program managers related to evaluation. Cheryl Holm-Hansen, a consulting scientist, supervises a unit that does internal evaluation. She describes strategic and operational features of her unit's work that increase the likelihood of delivering high-quality, useful information.

Role Within Wilder Research. On a day-to-day basis, the types of things in which the executive director might get involved regarding evaluation include:

> *Maintaining relationships with, and communicating to, the president and board of directors.* For example, I inform them about how we monitor our effectiveness and ask whether they want any changes in Wilder's evaluation approach. Recently, we discussed how our evaluation efforts fit with evidence-based practices and how we can better integrate our research findings with program operations to support improvement.
>
> *Preparing special reports for the board.* From time to time (especially for long-term issues), the board requests a special report, with a focus on service and outcomes. Sometimes the board has rated programs relative to one another.

Giving general advice and support. Research staff who implement internal evaluation occasionally seek advice regarding methods, stakeholder involvement, and other topics.

Recommending staff development. I recommend strategies to learn about issues that affect our work, competencies that staff should acquire, and tools that we should consider adopting. (In some cases, I lead discussions at meetings of research staff.)

Ensuring systems are in place. Managers of communications and finance report to me directly; I try to identify ways to improve the activities of all core units.

Promoting use. I look for ways to increase the use and usefulness of internal program evaluation. Sometimes, I develop a short publication or do a presentation; or I suggest steps others can take to get more findings into the hands of users. I also advise "point people" within Wilder Research (researchers who focus a portion of their efforts on a specific foundation priority area such as school success, troubled children).

Synthesizing. I sometimes look at evaluations of programs to synthesize lessons learned.

The Associate Director Perspective

We subscribe to a mission-driven orientation, and my work (coauthor Mueller) involves managing evaluation to carry out the missions of Wilder Research and the Wilder Foundation with organizations having purposes similar to the foundation's. Our orientation is to deliver services that enhance their ability to accomplish their mission. Success for us is being able to furnish them with useful information that they then use to improve program effectiveness.

Role Within Wilder Research. As associate director, I oversee most evaluation and other research activities. The research managers report to me, as well as the managers of the data collection, data analysis, and library core units. I am responsible for designing and implementing overall evaluation plans for Wilder programs, developing and implementing general policies and procedures to guide this work, ensuring that research staff have the necessary support to carry out evaluation efforts, and monitoring the quality of the work. I also identify and address general staff development needs related to conducting evaluation and other studies. Beyond these officewide management responsibilities, I also direct several evaluation and research studies.

Wilder Foundation. The foundation develops an overall evaluation plan and revises it periodically. I work with the executive in charge of Wilder programs and research managers within Wilder Research, whose teams lead the evaluations, to develop and revise the plan. The plan addresses the interests and priorities of program administrators (based on preliminary plans they develop with the research managers) and considers evaluation funding

NEW DIRECTIONS FOR EVALUATION • DOI: 10.1002/ev

available. It focuses on offering three types of data: participant outcomes, participant (or representative, such as a parent) satisfaction, and service accessibility. The plan typically contains corresponding objectives, measures, and performance targets. Funding cutbacks for evaluation in the past several years have resulted in fewer measurements of outcomes. Evaluation data are collected, analyzed, and reported, usually on an annual basis. Evaluation reports include recommendations for program improvement. After reports are completed, program and evaluation staff discuss the results and their implications. The overall evaluation plan also includes an evaluation of how well the foundation accomplishes its organizationwide strategic plan.

To illustrate my role in evaluation design, I will describe my efforts in designing an approach to evaluating progress made in accomplishing the strategic plan. As the foundation's strategic plan was taking shape, I began talking with the Wilder executive in charge of programs about how to approach evaluation of progress in implementing and achieving the goals of the strategic plan. We talked in person and by telephone several times. The executive favored an approach called the "balanced scorecard." This approach emphasizes regularly tracking progress on key "change initiatives" in the plan, using a set of indicators displayed in an easily accessible format.

I reviewed literature on the balanced scorecard approach to such an evaluation, including reading a book on its application to nonprofits or government agencies (Niven, 2003). The executive and I agreed that it offered a reasonable way to track progress on key initiatives vital to the success of the strategic plan. My draft of the evaluation design incorporated balanced scorecard ideas, including key "change" objectives for each major goal; initiatives to accomplish each objective; and indicators, measures, and targets to assess the progress in accomplishing each objective. For each change objective, I then formulated a more detailed evaluation design with measures and targets, based on business plans for each major strategic goal. Program managers and research managers reviewed the draft design several times; I made changes each time, until the design was then finalized.

Research managers, together with program staff, implemented this evaluation plan and measures within their respective foundation divisions. I monitor overall implementation of the plan including the timeline and budget. The research managers and I meet quarterly with the executive in charge of Wilder programs to review progress in implementing the evaluation design and discuss any issues that need attention. I prepare an annual report of results from the evaluation, with assistance from other staff.

Other Program Evaluation. I review selected program evaluation proposals of research staff, for studies in which I have a role or where my feedback may be helpful. In reviewing proposals, I look at how well the evaluation design will meet the needs of the client and other stakeholders and whether the evaluation will likely deliver results of practical use to program staff. Are the evaluation questions that are being posed the right ones, given the client's needs? How well do the proposed research methods address the evaluation questions? Is the evaluation likely to produce sound, useful findings that are actionable? I also look at the feasibility of the evaluation plan, including the time schedule and budget. I normally prepare written comments and meet with the researcher as needed.

Support and Quality Control in Conducting Program Evaluation. During each evaluation phase, specialists from Wilder Research core units assist research staff. These core units support the work of research staff, foster a standardized way of carrying out certain functions, and furnish quality monitoring. I meet regularly with the core unit managers I supervise to help shape their unit's services to meet the needs of the research staff and assist in resolving any problems that may arise.

To facilitate this process, we developed a checklist to remind research staff of the core units' services available during each phase of an evaluation project. For example, during the design phase research staff may request the literature search services supplied by the librarian to learn about the evaluations that have been done on similar programs and what methods were used, or they may seek advice on data collection methods from data collection unit staff. As the evaluation moves closer to implementation, data collection staff assist with instrument design and pretesting, translation of survey forms into other languages, and setting up the procedures for data collection. In the implementation phase, data collection staff coordinate and gather data through interviews, surveys, focus groups, records review, and so on. They clean the data and code data items, as needed. The data analysis unit staff review and comment on data collection protocols, enter the data, further clean the data, and store them. The research staff works with the data analysis staff to analyze the data. During the report-writing phase, communications and administrative support unit staff assist with report formatting, editing, and producing summaries or public versions of the report, as appropriate.

Quality checks occur during data collection, entry, analysis, and reporting. For example, 5–10 % of telephone interviews are monitored, programming for computer-assisted surveys enforces consistency, data entry checks occur, and staff review initial data runs for errors.

I regularly review Wilder evaluation reports and sometimes reports for outside clients before they are finalized. My review focuses especially on identifying the key findings, determining the strength of the evidence provided for them, and drawing out the implications of the findings for consideration by program staff and potential action to improve the program.

I meet with the data collection and data analysis unit managers every week or two. These meetings usually involve questions about a specific study, unit workload, personnel and staffing issues, or an issue that has arisen about some aspect of the services their unit provides. Examples of recent issues include quality of the coding of open-ended survey data, the system for monitoring telephone interviews, translation of surveys into other languages, and sampling design or procedures. In my meetings with core unit managers, I seek to understand each issue and offer guidance in how to deal with it, as needed. The manager and I may make an immediate decision or determine a strategy for resolving the issue, such as gathering more information about the issue or involving others in deciding what to do.

I also meet monthly with the librarian, who develops and makes available information services and resources that support the research staff. She and her staff maintain our library (which includes Wilder Research reports and other products or tools) and an electronic database of literature relevant to our work, do literature searches, obtain materials from outside libraries, circulate periodicals and newsletters, and post intranet information for designing and conducting evaluation (guidelines and tips for the stages and aspects of a study).

Over the years, we have developed written materials that provide guidance and standards to staff in conducting evaluation and other studies. The materials often emerge from internal staff trainings or from research staff discussions of an issue. The librarian includes many of them on our intranet page for easy access. For example:

- Proposal writing and budgeting guidelines
- Evaluation project design and set-up (such as logic model materials, estimating sample sizes, working with cultural groups different from one's own)
- Data collection (tips for creating an effective survey instrument, conducting focus groups)
- Writing reports and disseminating results (style standards, standards for reporting research results, developing a study communications plan)

Our communications/administrative support staff also developed a series of general templates that research staff use for evaluation reports, summaries, and presentations. These templates include the general Wilder Research format and style for these products.

Staff Development. In addition to the coaching and mentoring by senior research staff, we use several methods for internal staff development. First, we have monthly "research practice" meetings that all research staff attend. These meetings cover a variety of topics and issues relevant to evaluation and other studies. I organize these meetings and arrange for presenters or discussion leaders. Topics are usually suggested by research staff and are well grounded in our work. I base decisions regarding agenda topics on the importance of the issue to our work, timeliness, and interests of the research staff. Recent meeting topics included experimental and quasi-experimental design in evaluation studies, working effectively with clients, evaluation capacity building, sampling, developing contracts with clients, working effectively with Wilder Research core units, and communicating research results.

These sessions often lead to guidelines, tip sheets, or policies for our work, which we post on our intranet.

In addition to research practice meetings, I work with staff to organize informal sessions, usually over the lunch hour. Staff attend these sessions according to their interest and time available. These can include single training sessions or a series of sessions on such topics as proposal writing or appropriate use of various statistical techniques. These sessions can also be used to "practice" presenting research results prior to a more formal presentation, or to discuss and obtain ideas from colleagues on a challenging issue that has arisen in a study.

A monthly officewide staff meeting also affords an opportunity for staff to present research results in brief and longer formats, to further develop their skills.

Staff, of course, also participate in outside training and professional development opportunities.

The Research Manager Perspective

Role Within Wilder Research. As a consulting scientist at Wilder Research, I (coauthor Holm-Hansen) lead one of the research teams, manage my own evaluation and research projects, and supervise the work of six researchers with diverse educational backgrounds and professional experiences. In addition to monitoring projects, I work with each researcher to develop professional development goals and identify opportunities for pursuing these goals. I negotiate workloads and make project assignments. I am also responsible for revenue generation and fiscal management of the team. Finally, I participate in officewide management, serving on our administrative team.

Core Features of Our Approach. In selecting and completing projects, my goal is to ensure work conducted by my unit reflects several core features. As a manager, I want our projects to be:

> *Mission-driven.* Employees at all organizational levels consider this important. Many researchers work at Wilder Research due to its mission, and projects reflect our desire to perform work that will improve the social welfare of our community.
>
> *High-quality.* The integrity of our work also has vital importance, and we expect all projects to meet or exceed standards for research design, data collection, analysis, reporting, and ethical treatment of participants.
>
> *Feasible.* Most organizations with whom we partner have established timelines and budgets to accommodate. Feasibility and quality of the evaluation frequently need to be balanced against each other. At times, we decline projects because the timeline or budget prohibits

quality. More often, we make minor adjustments in our approach to ensure collection of the best possible information without time or cost overruns.

Useful. The staff at Wilder Research believe that the ultimate value of the evaluation lies in its usefulness. As described below, strategies and principles are woven throughout our work to enhance the ultimate usefulness of the research to a variety of stakeholders.

Promoting Use for Program Improvement. Virtually all of our projects are conducted in collaboration with community organizations, such as nonprofit agencies, school districts, and government entities. Although working in a collaborative framework is inherently more complex than working in isolation, it also yields higher-quality, and ultimately more useful, projects. Our goal at Wilder Research is to engage the community in a culture of evaluation, with our partners embracing evaluation as a vital program management strategy, rather than as an externally imposed requirement. We work in a conscious and intentional manner to promote evaluation as part of an ongoing process of program improvement.

Our desire to conduct evaluations that meaningfully inform program improvement permeates all aspects of our work. Though certainly not a comprehensive list, these examples describe features of our approach:

Focusing evaluation designs on program improvement process. Usefulness of the findings receives constant attention. A logic model helps us to develop a shared understanding of our partner agency's goals and activities, clarify their expectations for client outcomes, and identify and address underlying assumptions guiding their work. We attempt to identify the information needed by all project stakeholders, including staff, funders, consumers, and others. We work with stakeholders to identify the most important questions to be explored through the evaluation. Asking the most important questions increases our chances of providing the most important answers.

Developing positive relationships with agency staff. Evaluations proceed more smoothly, and the results receive more use, when agency staff and evaluators work as partners. Our staff work closely with client agencies and strive to create a nonthreatening relationship with them. Evaluation staff are encouraged to maintain a positive attitude, engage staff at multiple levels of the agency as appropriate, listen and respond fully and respectfully to staff concerns, and maintain ongoing communication. They also attempt to make available informal coaching and mentoring about the evaluation process, including what are they doing, why are they doing it, and how will it have an impact on the usefulness of the results.

Ensuring usefulness of reports. We make sure that the findings in every report are clear and understandable to a range of stakeholders.

NEW DIRECTIONS FOR EVALUATION • DOI: 10.1002/ev

Recommendations are reviewed to ensure that they are tied to the results, significant, and actionable. In each report, we highlight program strengths and identify areas of concern.

Identifying program improvement strategies. In some cases, we assist with program improvement strategies. When possible, we offer linkages to other research, reviewing results to inform our recommendations—what has worked in other programs to address shortcomings and identify potential avenues for improvement?

Overall Approach to Management. As a unit manager, I supervise a team of researchers. Our team meets once or twice a month to share updates on current projects and talk through challenges. My unit emphasizes a team approach. Each member serves as the lead consultant on several research projects, and we also help each other as needed. During team meetings, we discuss new projects, determining the best approach to take and assigning project leadership.

In addition to team meetings, I also meet individually with staff on a regular basis. We use both scheduled meetings and unscheduled discussions, typically talking about projects at least weekly. I also review written documents, including research plans, data collection materials, and reports. I offer feedback regarding organization, clarity, and usefulness.

Management Challenges. In supervising projects and managing a research unit, I face a number of challenges. Some challenges deal specifically with the process of conducting evaluations:

Managing evaluations in a context of program change. The agency environments in which we conduct evaluations often experience transitions. Changes in funding and staffing can alter the services offered, or lead to differing evaluation priorities. These transitions can challenge researchers who want to generate meaningful results, especially if the evaluations may not continue for enough time to derive significant findings. As a manager, I try to validate the frustrations of staff, while focusing on our role to support these agencies, ideally producing meaningful information to help them navigate transitions.

Meeting needs of staff at multiple levels within the organization. Researchers often partner with agencies that lack a shared vision regarding evaluation interests and priorities. Sometimes, agency leadership has different information needs from direct service staff. I try to support staff to identify the source and nature of conflicts and develop a strategy for successfully navigating them. Balancing competing stakeholder interests requires diplomacy. I support the researchers' efforts; in some cases, as supervisor, I step in to make difficult decisions, especially in situations where the researchers working directly with the program must maintain amicable relationships with agency staff.

NEW DIRECTIONS FOR EVALUATION • DOI: 10.1002/ev

Promoting an environment supportive of the evaluation. Not all agencies eagerly participate in evaluation. Sometimes agencies pursue evaluations to comply with funding requirements. Some programs seek solely to "look good" and avoid negative repercussions rather than ask important questions about service quality. Researchers must recognize these dynamics and engage unwilling partners in the evaluation process. Staff receive coaching to help identify and overcome resistance.

In addition to the challenges inherent in conducting useful community-based evaluations, I face other management challenges.

Promoting Staff Development. All research staff work with their supervisors to create a professional development plan. Most staff join Wilder Research with established skills related to research design and implementation; others are hired as students and gain research skills through experience. However, most staff need some formal training or informal coaching or mentoring to develop other skills. Three common themes emerge in professional development planning.

First, some staff require greater project management and business skills, such as proposal development, budgeting, project management, public speaking, and fiscal oversight. I try to offer gradual exposure to these activities and to increase their amount of independent management. For example, in terms of financial management, staff begin by simply monitoring costs on projects with established budgets. Staff then take responsibility for developing budgets and managing costs on relatively small projects. With success in this area, staff take responsibility for projects with increasingly larger budgets.

Second, some researchers need to develop confidence and general consulting competence to facilitate meetings, bring diverse stakeholders to consensus, and assess the political structure and interpersonal dynamics of the organizations with which they collaborate. Related to this, I usually begin by having staff attend meetings with me. Following each meeting, we debrief about the dynamics and my decisions about how to structure or manage the meeting. I encourage them to attend meetings with other senior researchers, so that they can see a number of management styles modeled. As staff begin to manage their own projects, I may accompany them to their meetings. Although I encourage them to facilitate these meetings, I remain available as a resource or step in if needed. Following each meeting, we share our perceptions of the meeting dynamics and identify strategies that were successful or unsuccessful in effectively managing the meeting. As staff gain experience and confidence, they attend meetings independently, though they may still talk to me about situations they face and potential strategies to consider in ensuring productive interactions with clients.

New Directions for Evaluation • DOI: 10.1002/ev

Third, some staff need to hone their research strengths to apply them more strongly to community-based research, requiring greater practice to prioritize evaluation questions, identify the most pertinent findings, and present meaningful recommendations for program improvement. I work with staff in these areas through ongoing formal meetings, informal discussions, and review of documents that they produce, such as evaluation designs, data collection tools, and reports.

Some staff require formal professional development opportunities, such as coursework or seminars. More often, learning occurs through informal mentoring and on-the-job experience. As a manager, I try to foster creative opportunities for staff to enhance skills and receive constructive feedback from colleagues and community collaborators.

Balancing Evaluation Quality With Staff Development Opportunities. As a manager, I want all of our clients to receive the highest-quality products. Simultaneously, I must balance the needs and interests of my staff, to give them opportunities to work on their preferred projects, including those that will help them to build the skills addressed in their professional development plans. To achieve this balance and offer staff meaningful learning opportunities in ways that will not detract from project quality, I supply additional supervision, behind the scenes guidance and oversight, and opportunities for novice staff to collaborate on projects with experienced staff.

Balancing Generalist Versus Specialist Orientations. All Wilder Research staff function as generalists, conducting evaluations and other research projects across a diverse array of content areas. Simultaneously, each researcher tends to have specific areas of interest in which he or she maintains content-area expertise. For example, my unit specializes in children's mental health and violence prevention. Other recent projects have addressed community revitalization, academic achievement among at-risk students, childhood obesity prevention, and alcohol and drug treatment.

I create opportunities for staff to work on projects that reflect their areas of interest and expertise. At the same time, I encourage them to think more generally about research and be aware of ways to use their skills effectively across a broad array of topics. Our librarian's services enhance the ability of staff to maintain their expertise and gain knowledge of unfamiliar areas.

Managing Multiple Evaluations Simultaneously. My seven-person research staff typically maintains an active project list of 30 to 40 evaluation and research studies. Each team member coordinates activities with others, as well as with the staff in other research units, to ensure that they meet timelines and do not overburden core units (e.g., data collection, data analysis). As a manager, I must know the general status of each project. Information sharing often occurs during regular team meetings, when we review the status of active projects, identify priorities for the following few weeks, and determine needs for core unit time. Between meetings, we maintain ongoing communication; I am available to review draft materials and help to resolve emerging implementation barriers. To balance the competing

NEW DIRECTIONS FOR EVALUATION • DOI: 10.1002/ev

needs of each unit, all research and core unit managers meet weekly to review active projects and support needs, and to negotiate if too much work is being requested of a unit.

Conclusion

This chapter describes our managing of evaluation within a large heterogeneous human services organization. This ongoing, evolving process requires substantive evaluation expertise in combination with strategic management and operations skills. For us, managing evaluation involves science plus people management, influenced by strategic principles that shape high-quality, cost-effective evaluation work—always guided by a mission to improve people's lives.

References

Aronovici, D. (1917). *Housing conditions in the City of Saint Paul.* Saint Paul, MN: Amherst H. Wilder Charity.

Davidoff, I., Guttentag, M., & Offutt, J. (Eds.). (1977). *Evaluating community mental health services: Principles and practice.* Rockville, MD: U.S. Department of Health, Education, and Welfare.

Mattessich, P. W. (2003). *The manager's guide to program evaluation.* St. Paul, MN: Amherst H. Wilder Foundation.

Niven, P, R. (2003). *Balanced scorecard step-by-step for government and nonprofit agencies.* Hoboken, NJ: Wiley.

Stockdill, S. H., Baizerman, M., & Compton, D. W. (2002). Toward a definition of the ECB process: A conversation with the ECB literature. In D.W. Compton, M. Baizerman, & S. H. Stockdill (Eds.), *The art, craft, and science of evaluation capacity building. New Directions for Evaluation, 93,* 7–25.

PAUL W. MATTESSICH *is executive director of Wilder Research in St. Paul, Minnesota.*

DANIEL P. MUELLER *is associate director of Wilder Research in St. Paul, Minnesota.*

CHERYL A. HOLM-HANSEN *is a consulting scientist at Wilder Research in Saint Paul, Minnesota; she also teaches college courses in human services and program evaluation.*

Rodosky, R. J., & Muñoz, M. A. (2009). Slaying myths, eliminating excuses: Managing for accountability by putting kids first. In D. W. Compton & M. Baizerman (Eds.), *Managing program evaluation: Towards explicating a professional practice. New Directions for Evaluation, 121,* 43–54.

4

Slaying Myths, Eliminating Excuses: Managing for Accountability by Putting Kids First

Robert J. Rodosky, Marco A. Muñoz

> What gets measured gets done.
> —*Peter F. Drucker*

Abstract

The authors write about evaluation, testing, and research and their relation to policy, planning, and program in the Jefferson County Public Schools (JCPS) in Louisville, Kentucky. The authors focus on evaluation and testing for accountability and on managing the unit for this purpose. In detail they show the many evaluation demands from both inside and outside JCPS, from the State of Kentucky to No Child Left Behind. Their everyday work context is active, often tumultuous. Managing evaluation in this context is a form of juggling, and the authors succeed in part because they "have seen most of it before." Also contributing to their effectiveness are the leaders' managing styles. This case study gives a good glimpse of the everyday life in a school district evaluation shop. © Wiley Periodicals, Inc.

This chapter is about managing for accountability in the large school system where I (Rodosky) have been the executive director of accountability, research, and planning for more than 25 years. Accountability for us means that schools, teachers, parents, central office

administrators, and the community must be held responsible for the education of the district's children. Over the years, I have co-created structures and processes to support ongoing evaluation for accountability, program improvement, decision making, and meeting external and internal mandates.

My job is everyday managing of the structures and processes of our data-driven work to meet external and internal mandates and to supply data for school and community decision making. I come to work each day knowing what has to be produced for whom, by whom, when, and how; I have great confidence that my staff will do their work and their products will be right—in subject, timing, truthfulness, and the like.

Writing from the perspective of being at work on an ordinary day, I tell you how I manage for accountability through deliverables, processes, and practices; staff and budgetary concerns; and everyday politics. The structures and processes are in place, and my stance is that of facilitator decision maker, "excuse eliminator," coach, cheerleader, and politician. I conclude with reflections on my beliefs and values and how they guide my everyday management of this complex system, and a discussion of the essential practices of managing evaluation for accountability in a large urban school system.

Context for Our Accountability Work

When I begin my day at 7:00 a.m., I know what I have to get done and know too that something unexpected is likely to emerge. I know what projects staff are working on, when the work is due, what likely problems they will encounter, and how I will no doubt respond.

JCPS is located in Louisville, Kentucky; it is the 31st largest district in the nation with an urban core, suburban housing, and diminishing rural areas. It has 150 schools serving approximately 98,000 students, with an annual budget of more than $1 billion. It has about 13,700 full-time and 5,800 part-time employees. The district has a student assignment plan based on "managed choice," which facilitates racial desegregation of its schools by furnishing students with transportation from their neighborhood home to another part of the district. This plan has been the focus of extensive court examination up to the present time.

School-Based Decision Making (SBDM) is part of the Kentucky Education Reform Act (KERA) of 1990, and individual SBDM teams set school policy consistent with district board policy, while district officials can suggest academic programs and interventions. Individual schools, through SBDM, have ultimate control over adoption of curricula and programs in their building.

There is an elected board of education, a superintendent, and one assistant superintendent for each school level. Accountability, Research, and Planning is one of 10 departments that report directly to the superintendent. We have 22 employees focused on delivering reliable, valid, and useful information to decision makers in a timely manner.

NEW DIRECTIONS FOR EVALUATION • DOI: 10.1002/ev

Student learning development is the schools' primary purpose. To monitor and assess this purpose, the district tracks and reports academic progress regularly through multiple reports, such as District Report Card, School Reports Cards, No Child Left Behind (NCLB), Adequate Yearly Progress (AYP) results, and an online database of student formative assessments. From the perspective of data use and continuous improvement, I believe that diagnostic, formative assessment is equally valuable as summative assessment results. As a result, we keep a balance in our district between multiple types of assessments.

Internal Organization for Delivering Our Evaluation Work. The department includes research, planning, and accountability. The Research Unit carries out institutional research and data warehousing activities and promotes district internal and external research and evaluation activities by generating valid, reliable, and timely data, efficiently and in an atmosphere that is inviting, receptive, and responsive to the data needs of its customers in the schools and community. It also designs, administers, and reports surveys giving feedback for planning and evaluating programs to the board of education and local schools. These annual surveys are designed from a whole-child educational framework and to assess satisfaction with our educational services. This unit conducts its own research activities and acts as a clearinghouse for external research initiatives, providing initial screening and support to a variety of research requests.

Second is the Planning Unit, which coordinates state-required school and district plans and offers service to the district for its Southern Association of Colleges and Schools (SACS) accreditation. The Planning Unit coordinates the format, timelines, quality reviews, and training for development of the Comprehensive School Improvement Plan (CSIP). It also compiles the Comprehensive District Improvement Plan (CDIP), which outlines proposed work improvements in the core content areas of reading, writing, and mathematics. The CDIP also lays out a district plan to allocate resources to its most struggling schools, while also coordinating the district's dialogue and coaching process on priority schools (i.e., low-performing schools) identified through assessment data. Finally, the unit offers grant writing technical support and evaluation services to numerous district grants and programs for use in program improvement.

The third area is accountability (testing). The Testing Unit focuses on coordination, implementation, and management of logistics associated with the various state and district assessments. We use both statewide academic and nonacademic assessments, and a district-based continuous assessment process, along with several other assessment programs, all with their own rules, instruments, and timing. All of our research, planning, and accountability work is contextual, and some of this is discussed next.

External Influences on Our Evaluation Work. Federal mandates influencing our work include the Elementary and Secondary Education Act

(ESEA) Title I program and NCLB. The latter requires specific evaluation of Annual Measurable Objectives (AMOs)—a task that has created much work.

At the state level, KERA (1990) requires regular district assessments of student academic and nonacademic performance.

Other laws, external requirements, and data demands drive our work. Given the uniqueness of our district, this makes it difficult to meet these often competing demands.

Structural Location. The structural, organizational location of the Accountability, Research, and Planning Department is critical to its effectiveness. It is crucial to have direct-line reporting to the superintendent, particularly when everyone comes to us for data requests from inside and outside the schools. As manager, I influence priorities, what does and does not get done, evaluation designs, cost, and timelines. I deal with internal and external "gatekeepers," and I have a data dissemination role within and outside the district; that is, I serve as the district's data contact for community-based children's and youth services.

To be effective, I must have authority to carry out these complex tasks and a direct line to the superintendent. In our data-based, accountability-focused world, having such authority is vital.

Our customers are inside and outside the schools, including community-based organizations. For example, we have developed partnerships with more than 70 community groups who use our online data system to tutor, counsel, and mentor students.

The Work: Our Accountability Department and Deliverables

Our district and department have systems and processes in place to respond to accountability demands. Our work is guided by our mission to facilitate data-based decision making. We use primarily Stufflebeam's Context-Input-Process-Product (CIPP) Model (Stufflebeam et al., 1971) to give users practical, valid, reliable, and timely data. I am especially excited about our Web-based data reporting, which uses point-and-click designs making fresh data available to all stakeholders.

Deliverables. My department produces multiple reports for the superintendent, administrators, and the board of education. For the superintendent, each evaluation report is composed of three sections: an executive summary, a managerial report, and a technical report. The executive summary concisely describes key elements of the full evaluation report: (1) background information, (2) evaluation questions, (3) evaluation method and instrumentation, (4) evaluation findings, and (5) evaluation recommendations. The managerial report presents more detailed information focused more on processes than outcomes; it is written for a nontechnical audience. The third is the technical report, which gives detailed statistics. These are often presented at national conferences or published in peer-reviewed journals.

Key deliverables in our district are two locally produced books, *School Profiles* and *Data Books,* with multiple academic and nonacademic data aggregated at the school level. They summarize the comprehensive demographic, cognitive, and noncognitive characteristics and achievement of each school and the district as a whole.

Comprehensive school surveys are another basic deliverable. We develop, distribute, administer, collect, analyze, and report on feedback surveys from various stakeholders (students, parents, teachers, staff) about school and district practices. Areas covered by these surveys weave together the threads that connect not only reading, writing, math, science, social studies, practical living, and arts/humanities, but also the important social-emotional, civic, and moral connections that tend to be fragmented in our more test-driven, accountability-oriented approach. We know that children do not develop and learn in isolation, but rather grow physically, socially, emotionally, ethically, and intellectually within networks of families, schools, neighborhoods, communities, and our larger society. Without a doubt, these surveys call for a paradigm shift in how schools and communities look at our children's learning, putting the whole child at the center of decision making.

Our new deliverable is a formative assessment system using new technologies to produce results. For example, teachers can produce individual student test answer sheets aligned with district-made benchmark tests and Web-based "dashboard" reports.

Data for Decision Making. The superintendent and board of education need data for policymaking. Some come directly from the state department of education, but we generate, analyze, and report most of what they want and use. We develop our teacher decision-making data. Because most summative reports are not useful for classroom teachers deciding on instructional steps for individual students, we developed a system of formative assessments with a variety of measures that generate school-, class-, and student-level data for use by teachers, counselors, and principals.

In general, data from state and district assessments are moved electronically into the district's system and are readily available to teachers for planning instruction and making curricular decisions. Student data from multiple assessments are individually entered into the system (either by keyboard entry or scanning) and available for teacher use.

All of these timely, easily accessible data allow district leadership, principals, staff members, parents, community members, and SBDM council to analyze student performance in an individual school, determine progress toward CSIP goals and benchmarks, and evaluate the effectiveness of the district's or school's interventions and programs.

Planning. District organizational improvement is another focus. We help answer questions about the mission of the schools and our department, and what must be done to remain competitive. This is ever more crucial because public schools are no longer a monopoly, competing with private and parochial schools for students (that is, market share). Data are basic to our mission of moving market share from our current 80% to our goal of 100%.

Basic to organizational development is identification and assessment of best practices across the country. We help decision makers with data on these practices and help also with long-range planning, generating reports about finances, operations, and the external environment. Additionally, we help school- and community-based planning by collecting, analyzing, and using data.

Evaluation. Evaluation is a core component of my everyday work. Using the Joint Committee Standards for Program Evaluation (1994) as a guide, we go about evaluating key initiatives and programs to ensure that we are helping our students.

We use the CIPP model (Stufflebeam et al., 1971) of evaluations of context, inputs, processes, and products. *Context-evaluations* assess needs and opportunities to help decision makers define objectives and priorities. *Input evaluations* assess alternative approaches and strategies for their feasibility and cost-effectiveness to meet identified needs. Decision makers use input evaluations in choosing among competing plans, writing funding proposals, allocating resources, and organizing work. *Process evaluations* assess implementation of plans to help staff carry out activities and help stakeholders improve program performance. *Product evaluations* identify and assess outcomes, intended or unintended.

We have an evaluation team to develop structures and processes to offer useful information to support student learning. It establishes results-oriented learning processes, and data are used for practical improvement of schools and classrooms. The evaluation team develops a program profile (including the program's goals), conducts evaluation processes and activities, and reports evaluation results and recommendations to key stakeholders. During the evaluation process, evaluators visit all schools involved, observe classrooms, and interview students and teachers.

Throughout the evaluation, academic data are used to assess progress toward improvement in student learning targets. The evaluation team makes recommendations about the future of each program, including reduction, expansion, elimination, adjustment, and status quo maintenance. Clearly, evaluation is central to our department's work on accountability.

So too is communicating about what we do, how we do it, and what we have learned. Our message has a purpose and an audience: promoting decision making based on valid, reliable, and timely data. Our messages teach by storytelling and through casual conversation. However, the storytelling and casual conversations are based on empirical data!

Community Change. Our district promotes community change by collecting, analyzing, and producing data to inform decision making on the part of community service agencies that offer programs to children and youths. For example, we regularly stay involved with community-based organizations (CBOs) and other not-for-profits working toward the community's and schools' mission of serving our kids.

Reciprocally, we receive many kinds of support from partner organizations. In collaboration with Vanderbilt University, we help facilitate a capstone project for advanced graduate students doing the Ed.D. We are now helping the University of Louisville create a new Ed.D. program oriented toward practitioners that will include an inquiry-based pedagogy, laboratories of practice, and a bias toward action.

Day-to-Day Managing: Ways of Producing the Evaluation Work

The most fundamental aspect of day-to-day managing for accountability is that you must know for whom you work. I have a sign outside my door saying that we work for our superintendent in his or her efforts to deliver the best instruction and services to students. To carry out this mission, the superintendent gives me full authority to execute my responsibilities. Within this framework, we strive always to produce a quality product within a specified timeline and budget. How I structure and manage the daily operations of my department is driven by a focus on outcomes that benefit kids— it's as simple as that.

Structure and Processes. The basic structure of the Accountability, Research, and Planning Department is organized around outcomes. Our bottom line is customer service focused on student learning. The department's delivery system operates on well-defined objectives organized within a framework that is both vertically and horizontally aligned. The vertical alignment comes directly from our superintendent; the chain of command from him to my staff and me is clearly established and concerned with the flow of authority and responsibility. Horizontal alignment arises from my knowing the strengths and weaknesses of my departmental team.

A variety of structures and processes help us deliver accountability data, analyses, and reports related to our accountability, research, and planning functions. These processes require constant monitoring to ensure timely delivery. If we are doing the same work in the same way, over a period of several years, we are probably inefficient and insufficient. I keep in regular contact with exemplary agencies to benchmark our activities.

We set objectives for all structures and processes. These are specific, feasible, measurable, and time-bound. We include key stakeholders in these discussions; this meets the Standards for Program Evaluation requirement of stakeholder involvement. It also gives us an opportunity to create buy-in with key staff and stakeholders and objectives that are truly based on stakeholders' needs and wants. Additionally, we keep a sharp focus on the needs of our customers and continuously reassess whether discrepancies exist between what is and what is desired. The objectives of all our structures and processes must satisfy the needs of our key customer base: our students!

NEW DIRECTIONS FOR EVALUATION • DOI: 10.1002/ev

When seen as a process of development, strong leadership is critical in the early phases of developing new structures and processes. Leadership to me is about moving beyond mere management. My work as a manager is not only to carry out our policies and procedures but to create more efficient structures and processes. This process is guided by a vision that comes from my colleagues at the top of the organization as to how to respond to the changing environment of public education.

Other fundamental issues associated with structure and processes include a strong belief in delegation; I call this "Attend for Bob," or AFB—staff members representing me can make commitments about projects and work plans without getting prior approval. I have the utmost confidence in my staff's judgment because low-maintenance staff surround me. They know each other's strengths and weaknesses for task assignments, and they maintain high professional standards. All of these elements can be understood within the frame of me as "Excuse Eliminator."

Staff. We hire only the best people, and our staff can analyze data with sophisticated statistical techniques and also develop data systems easily accessed on the Web. More important, my staff are trustworthy. They can represent the department in meetings, make decisions about technical aspects of their work, and meet the other requirements of evaluation research without being micromanaged.

I ensure that staff are always up to date with professional and organizational knowledge and skills, including new technology; our very high-quality evaluation work is seen in professional presentations and publications.

I use my involvement in the Consortium for Research on Accountability and Teacher Education (CREATE) to enhance collaboration between my staff and professionals from highly regarded school districts and universities, among them Northwestern, Vanderbilt, the University of Louisville, the University of Kentucky, Dallas Independent School District, and Western Michigan University. This keeps them interested and contributes to job and personal enrichment and development of these knowledge workers.

As a site of excellence, we also have full- and part-time interns. We are a laboratory of practice where the students apply their tools with real-life problems and under the supervision of our senior researchers.

Staff are critical to promoting improved services to students and schools. My job is to furnish the enabling conditions; I am, as I suggested, an Excuse Eliminator. I constantly ask staff, "What do you need to get the work done in a quality and timely way?" I support new developments if they make sense and will likely better serve our customers. I work to create the space for my staff to envision and implement alternative organizational structures and processes. My bias is toward action, through trial and error, and always with our kids in mind. We are productive simply because I have a competent and hard-working staff. Managing day-to-day means allowing and supporting them to do their best; that's my job!

Budget. My philosophy is that the work precedes the budget. I believe that we need to work smarter rather than harder (Drucker, 2006). This extends to how we use funds. In any given year, we typically receive the same amount of funding as in the previous year. I use my flexibility in crossing accounting codes to avoid asking for extra funding. Why? Because in school districts, the more you ask for, the more you will become a target for cost reductions.

We need to constantly rethink what is necessary to better respond to new needs within budget constraints. This is the true test of the efficiency and productivity of our system, not whether our budget is larger.

Because of my project management experience, I budget the cost of processes associated with the work, including data acquisition, input, storage, analysis, and reporting. If truly necessary, I seek additional funds to make specific studies happen. Why? Because staff need to have what is required to do their work. My job is to ensure that my people have what they must to be successful. I use several strategies to bring in additional funds, directly or in-kind. One way is by creating partnerships with schools and other departments through joint projects. My operational rule is that schools or departments have to match (at some level, but usually 10–25%) our financial support.

My budget always includes funding for professional development activities and for technology, both of which are basic support elements for our work in planning, research, evaluation, and accountability. These line items, which are a target for cuts in some organizations, are the last to be considered when we have to give up funding, for the reasons just discussed. Without top staff and good, appropriate technology, we simply could not do our work.

Politics. We are all at JCPS for the common purpose of helping kids reach a high level of achievement so they can learn to their fullest potential and live successful lives after graduation. We exist to investigate whether this is happening and to suggest ways of reaching these basic goals. Such social goals have also come to be seen as our community's shared political goals. My department's job is to help principals, teachers, students, and administrators meet these larger goals by using appropriate data correctly.

I try to do this in ways that avoid the appearance of taking sides. One form of taking sides relates to the boundaries between personal and professional friendships. I do not have lunch or socialize with certain stakeholders. I must be transparent in my work of supplying good and useful data for decision making. I want to be known for being a highly knowledgeable and skilled individual of integrity who helps everybody and is not a broker of information for self-promotion or to prove my importance.

Politics by its nature is woven into the fabric of everyday life. As a manager, I have to be clear about the chain of command in my organization.

I work for the superintendent. We receive direction from him and share with him findings in response to requests for information from internal and external customers, including members of the board of education.

On the community side, politics are reflected in education, curriculum, and school structure. The SBDM councils give principals, teachers, and parents power to make important decisions about how their school is operated and how the teaching and learning processes therein will be done. At the same time, the school is accountable for learning outcomes.

In summary, there are "politics" and there are politics, and in all of JCPS and in our community and state there are both kinds and more. This is quite typical of public education, school bureaucracies, and the work of accountability, evaluation, and research because each can be used for political (partisan) ends. We try our best to be nonpartisan and available to all sides in any political issue or policy or programmatic controversy and debate.

Reflections: Guidance for Managing Evaluation for Accountability

One needs core beliefs and values to guide one's everyday work. For me, these beliefs and values work as touchstones for what to do and how to build and manage evaluations and evaluators for accountability. I believe that my group and I must be morally accountable for our work.

I believe in an open door, customer service orientation to those inside and outside the schools. My internal customers are the superintendent and the assistant superintendents, board members, executive directors, and program coordinators. But my most important internal customers are students, teachers, and parents. My external customers are the local, state, and federal leaders interested in developing our public schools. This is department policy, and this philosophy is found in all the ways in which we respond to all of our customers.

I also believe in data-based decision making. To that end, I continuously work to bring empirical data to all relevant work conversations. I resist talking in terms of perception-based hunches. I slay myths with data! For me, this is a core value.

I also believe that ad hoc work, if proven, should become business as usual. I work on this constantly. One example was development of the school profiles and data books. In some years, I would receive several requests from community members, parents, principals, and other school staff for the same information. I had to respond to each request, an inefficient use of my time. As a result, we built a process to generate a consistent response (that is, institutionalizing routines). We now produce these books early in the school year. In this way, we created a needed, useful product and turned the ad hoc into a regular and recurring process.

I also believe in recruiting and hiring the best people, as was previously described. I value this most highly as a manager. The right individual in an evaluation unit means someone who is capable of analyzing and improving his or her own work (meta-evaluation).

I believe that it is important to stay up-to-date with major issues associated with accountability, assessment, and evaluation in the schools and the community. I do this through regular involvement in CREATE and in professional organizations such as the American Educational Research Association (AERA) and the American Evaluation Association (AEA).

These core values most influence how I manage evaluation. All are involved in my recommendations for best practices.

Essential Practices of Evaluation for Accountability

The essential and best practices of my evaluation for accountability involve multiple elements: (1) a passion for kids as a moral grounding; (2) credibility when presenting results (both good and bad); (3) a trifocal perspective (the tree, the forest, and the interconnectedness of the two); (4) a polychronic structure (multiple clocks all keeping the school calendar in mind); (5) a transparent, democratic process (eliminate gate keeping); (6) data-driven policy decision making; and (7) self-reflection while comparing oneself constantly against best practices.

A passion for kids is naturally the core element here. If you don't like kids, as far as I am concerned, you are in the wrong business! Evaluation for accountability in the school setting means helping kids.

Credibility is another important element, the coinage of the realm. It is precious and must be husbanded carefully. I do honest work and can defend my work. I do not tilt, edit, or in any way distort data.

Another core element I use is trifocal lenses to view my work. When examining an issue, I make sure to look from both concrete/unique and abstract/general perspectives. I also must see the synergy and interrelations between the individual and the systemic.

I bring a polychronic perspective to decision making and organizational processes. There are multiple "watches" ticking in my mind when it comes down to decision making. For example, I build my work around the school calendar. I know there are some decisions that need to be made in March (such as planning, funding), some during the summer months, some at the beginning of the school year, and some at the semester break. This is unavoidable in a large school system when one is evaluating for accountability.

I like to eliminate gate keeping through creation of a transparent, democratic process that facilitates access to data. This access to data, in turn, facilitates my ultimate goal: sustaining a data-driven decision-making environment.

Last, I am and must be self-reflective because I am accountable for my work as a manager and for my department's productivity. Self-reflection is my self-evaluation; my work is also data-driven! At the end of the day or the school year, I am responsible.

Conclusion

For managers of evaluation for accountability, it is important to not forget essential practices such as one's credibility, keeping a multifocal and multi-chronic perspective, keeping data work transparent and democratic, supporting data-driven policy decision making, and engaging in ongoing self-reflection. Basic to all of this is the simple philosophical and moral base of our work: Kids must always come first. Second is using data for accountability and other purposes. The best manager of this work will be the one whose job it is to eliminate any kind of excuse that gets in the way of producing accurate, meaningful, credible, useful data.

My hope is that new generations of managers of evaluation for accountability will continue to put kids first and not fall into believing that our work as evaluators is more important than the teacher's work in the classroom. Our work is a means and support toward an end: student learning. Our job is to support teachers and principals as they work to accomplish the most precious work of all: educating children so they can become well-rounded lifelong learners and contributors in the crucial process of making a better world.

References

Drucker, P. F. (2006). *Classic Drucker: Essential wisdom of Peter Drucker from the pages of Harvard Business Review*. Boston,: Harvard Business Press.

The Joint Committee on Standards for Educational Evaluation. (1994). *The program evaluation standards: How to assess evaluations of educational programs*. Thousand Oaks, CA: Sage.

Stufflebeam, D. L., Foley, W. J., Gephart, W. J., Hammond, L. R., Merriman, H. O., & Provus, M. M. (1971). *Educational evaluation and decision-making in education*. Itasca, IL: Peacock.

ROBERT J. RODOSKY *is the executive director of the Accountability, Research, and Planning Department for the Jefferson County Public Schools in Louisville, Kentucky.*

MARCO A. MUÑOZ *is an evaluation specialist in the Accountability, Research, and Planning Department of the Jefferson County Public Schools.*

NEW DIRECTIONS FOR EVALUATION • DOI: 10.1002/ev

Compton, D. W. (2009). Managing studies versus managing for evaluation capacity building. In D. W. Compton & M. Baizerman (Eds.), *Managing program evaluation: Towards
explicating a professional practice. New Directions for Evaluation, 121,* 55–69.

5

Managing Studies Versus Managing for Evaluation Capacity Building

Donald W. Compton

Abstract

*Donald W. Compton, the first director of evaluation services at the National Home
Office (Atlanta) of the American Cancer Society, tells the story of building the unit
in conditions of high demand and a limited budget. Along the way, evaluation was
brought to regional divisions and to local offices in part as a response to United
Way and to his work organizing training. The strategy for unit development and
for sustaining the work was the Collaborative Evaluation Fellows Project. This
proved to be an effective strategy of building evaluation capacity (ECB), then a
newly conceptualized model of evaluation managing. Compton tells about the
work and draws lessons for managing ECB.* © Wiley Periodicals, Inc.

Getting to ECB

As the first director and only staff person of the first evaluation unit at the
National Home Office (NHO) of the American Cancer Society (ACS) in
1995, my first 6 months were spent meeting with NHO staff, learning what
evaluation they wanted, and learning about ACS cultures and how and
where decisions were made. I also worked at creating a network of colleagues inside and outside ACS to help me think through how to try to

make evaluation a regular and routine part of ACS's work at NHO and nation-wide. After these conversations, I came to believe that I had to work at three levels: with the NHO, with top leadership and program staff at the ACS's 17 regional offices, and with nearby Atlanta ACS staff and volunteers. After three months of unsuccessfully trying to schedule a meeting with the local regional CEO, my supervisor recommended that I ask an ACS executive vice president for operations (EVP) to schedule the meeting to discuss submitting a grant proposal to a local foundation. The idea was to join ACS national and regional offices with nearby schools of public health to conduct practical, use-ful, and timely evaluation using graduate students under faculty supervision. Both my immediate supervisor and the EVP supported the idea. By then I knew that I also needed the support of the 17 regional CEOs if the proposal were to be funded and implemented in real and practical ways.

The Atlanta regional CEO met us and, after he and the EVP reviewed the agenda for a meeting they were co-chairing, he told us about his morn-ing with the CEO of the Atlanta-area United Way. In general, ACS had a his-tory of successful funding by United Way. For this to continue, he had been told ACS would be required to submit logic models and outcome data demonstrating the success of their regional and local programs. As he described this meeting, questions ran through my head: What would I do if he asked for my help on this? How could ACS nationwide respond to these demands from United Ways around the country, with me as the only eval-uation staff? How could ACS produce outcome data since there was no sys-tematic process in place to collect them, much less analyze the data and prepare reports? How could ACS staff develop logic models if they had lit-tle if any understanding of a logic model and how it might be used? With these questions flying around my head, the CEO asked me what I would recommend that he do, and he asked whether I could help his staff respond to this new United Way demand.

After asking about the types and number of his programs, I said to the EVP, "What if we told him about our idea to join ACS offices to schools of public health to do usable evaluation studies? That could be a practical and low-cost way to furnish him with evaluation expertise to respond to United Way." Both the EVP and the regional CEO discussed whether ACS was developing other proposals for this particular foundation, and whether it was practical and politically feasible to consider putting forward our pro-posal at the next meeting of national and regional leadership. Knowing ACS politics, the regional CEO, was skeptical and said that he did not think CEOs nationwide would move evaluation to the top of their wish list. At the same time, he thought the idea was worth pilot-testing and agreed to allo-cate $6,000 to fund a graduate student and faculty to evaluate their local Reach to Recovery program for breast cancer patients.

As he talked, my face turned into a smile, and I moved forward in my chair. Maybe this was going to happen yet! At the same time, a wave of fear shot through me as I realized I had my first evaluation funding from a regional office. Now I had to make this work! I had to figure out how to help them build their capacity to do and use evaluation studies. Then I had to do this throughout the three ACS levels: nationwide, regionally, and locally. Thus was born evaluation capacity building (ECB). One of its shapes was the Collaborative Evaluation Fellows Project (CEFP).

The purpose of this article is to present a case example of managing ECB, a process long practiced but only recently named, illuminated, and explicated (Compton, Baizerman, & Stockdill, 2002). ECB is a structure as well as a related, joined process, and managing them is a qualitatively different practice than managing a single study, a set of evaluations, a group of evaluators, or an evaluation unit. It is a different practice but related to managing for program improvement and for program accountability, both of which can be subsumed under ECB.

The strategy is to tell the story of building an evaluation unit. It is a narrative of a first director moving from being overwhelmed by evaluation demand and the potential for substantive, meaningful, usable evaluation for accountability and program improvement, to creating structures and processes that later came to be called ECB. After ECB is analyzed as a new evaluation focus and practice, concluding sections discuss managing for ECB and its guiding principles.

Organizational and Social Context of the ACS (1995–2002)

The ACS is now a 95-year-old, nationwide, voluntary health organization. It is the largest nongovernmental organization (NGO) in the nation, with approximately two million volunteers. According to its mission statement, ACS is dedicated to eliminating cancer as a major health problem by preventing cancer, saving lives, and diminishing suffering from cancer through research, education, advocacy, and service (http://www.cancer.org). The organization has set challenge goals for reducing the age-adjusted cancer incidence rate by 24% and age-adjusted cancer mortality rate by 50% by the year 2015. Funds come primarily from individual donations, corporate philanthropy, and United Way. The NHO is in Atlanta, Georgia, and between 1995 and 2002 there were 17 regional offices and 3,400 community-level offices when our ECB effort was developed and implemented.

Historically, ACS devoted little systematic effort to determining program effectiveness. Until 1995, a small number of evaluation studies were contracted to external evaluators to study volunteer, staff, and program participants' experiences and opinions. Routine data collection involved counting the number of program participants or activities, without measuring outcomes or goal achievement. In this, ACS was typical of large (and small) national NGOs in health and social services.

ACS was pressed by both internal and external demands, locally and nationally, for program evaluation. It responded by hiring one person, who was called director, evaluation services, at its NHO. I began my work by visiting colleagues throughout the NHO to assess their needs and wants for evaluation. Soon it became clear that NHO staff were willing to use the in-house evaluation service, overwhelming the one-person, no-budget operation; latent and induced demand outstripped capacity. Also present was an imperative to educate ACS staff about professional evaluation practice and its guiding principles, and to explain the contrast between this approach and others grounded in social marketing, communications, economics, accounting, management science, and especially experimental research and epidemiology—more typical ACS strategies. Few NHO, regional office, or local ACS staff had professional evaluation training or contacts with professional evaluators in the community, at local universities, or at the Centers for Disease Control and Prevention (CDC). Further, there were major infrastructure changes at ACS at the same time, including the mergers of state offices into regional offices, changes in national and regional board structures and functions, and changing roles for volunteers. Evaluation arrived at the moment the NHO and local offices were being "shaken up."

At the same time, the United Way, an important source of funding for most local ACS offices, began to require local affiliates to implement and use evaluation logic models and outcome measurement. This requirement for outcome evaluation quickly, and often abruptly, awakened ACS to the fact that their local programs had to be evaluated if they were receiving United Way funds. No agencywide process or resources existed to respond locally or nationally to these demands. In addition, ACS was benefiting from the country's general economic well-being by also receiving substantial donations from individuals and was under public pressure from them to demonstrate accountability and program effectiveness (Compton, Glover-Kudon, Avery, & Morris, 2001).

Given the changes in ACS at the national, regional, and local levels; increasing demands for accountability and proof of effectiveness at the three levels; and the absence of agency policy, structure, staff, and devoted fiscal resources, I was in the position of either walking away from the chaos or finding ways to respond to it. I chose to stay, and I will describe next what I did to implement an agencywide response.

Toward a Departmental Vision. After only a few months in my new position and with the relentless demand for evaluation services becoming a routine part of the job, I struggled with several key questions:

- How do I shape the NHO demand for evaluation so that professional evaluators would understand what is needed and be able to respond? For example, because of the ACS staff's extremely limited understanding of evaluation, expectations for studies were vague, unclear, and unrealistic.
- Where will I find the professional evaluators to do this work?

- Who will pay for the work since my department has no budget for evaluation studies?
- How can I work to ensure that the evaluation is practical, useful, and timely and will be used for program improvement and other purposes?
- How can I as a person manage a significant number of multiple and simultaneous national, regional, and local evaluations?
- How can I work to make sure evaluation and its uses become a regular and ongoing part of ACS at all levels?
- How can I garner support from ACS leadership for the evaluation function and use of evaluation reports in their policy formulation and programmatic decision making?

As I reflected on these questions, it was clear that I would be unable to develop a plan to respond without help from experienced colleagues who understood not only professional evaluation but ACS's organizational context and how evaluation might become integrated into all levels of the organization. I talked with colleagues nationwide to get perspectives on how to respond; on the basis of my experience in the educational system, with its highly formalized evaluation structures and processes, I decided that the first thing to do was to create formal structures and processes as a step toward building the long-term future of evaluation, as well as a way to deal with the massive actual and potential workload.

In retrospect, CEFP was the broad instrument within which we invented, tested, implemented, and evaluated a family of strategies that later came to be called ECB. However, in the living moment of 1995, all that was clear was that I needed some systematic way to prioritize and respond to NHO demand for evaluation. One way to do this quickly and at no cost to the Evaluation Services budget was to persuade ACS program managers to fund the evaluations, and for me to find outside contract evaluators who would produce high-quality, practical, useful, and timely work. This meant contacting colleagues at the American Evaluation Association in Texas, Virginia, and Minnesota. They would do studies while I worked at designing and implementing structures and processes for systematically contracting external evaluators. This left open the issue of building demand at local ACS offices, which were increasingly aware of evaluation because of what were then new demands for outcome data from their primary funder, United Way of America. Obviously, this potential demand would also need a model for contracting and managing external contractors.

The first structure I moved to develop was for contracting external evaluators. I also advocated for four additional staff: one senior professional evaluator, two junior professional evaluators, and one support person.

At the same time, it became surprisingly clear that local ACS offices did not typically have close working relationships to locally based schools of public health. Some university-based consultants in land grant institutions, with their tradition of community service, suggested that faculty-supervised students from local university departments teaching evaluation practice (such as public health, education) could be a good source of relatively low-cost evaluators, while simultaneously building long-term relationships with local ACS offices and with me at the NHO. The potential here was for ACS to become a training site for evaluators who then could be hired by ACS to meet the increasing internal and external demand at least for evaluation for accountability and program improvement. Given this broad vision for evaluation within ACS, I wondered how I could bring it about. The next chapter in this story of developing evaluation at ACS and developing what came to be called ECB was inventing programmatic space—developing the CEFP.

Implementing the Vision as CEFP

If the vision were to be realized, I would need resources, power, and time. The basic idea was simple: join ACS to universities and external contractors to offer evaluation services to ACS on the national and local levels. In this way, my one-person unit would become as large a staff as necessary. The story I tell is about the university connection. It came to be called the CEFP. ACS asked for and received support for this from the Robert W. Woodruff Foundation in Atlanta. CEFP was a collaborative effort between ACS and university-based schools of public health. It was an ECB strategy for delivering evaluation services to the ACS at all levels, that is, doing much of ACS's evaluation work.

The basic notion of CEFP was to match and integrate complementary needs and resources of ACS and schools of public health. It was a perceived win-win proposition for both because ACS had high evaluation needs and limited evaluation resources, and the schools of public health had a large number of graduate students interested in real-world practical evaluation experience under faculty supervision but few paid supervised experiences. The project also was an opportunity for university faculty to test their theories and evaluation models in real-world settings. The ACS evaluation unit wanted to show ACS at the national level how evaluation could contribute to improved programs and services, and meet demands for accountability. More than 150 evaluation projects were completed in 22 universities over 5 years, involving almost 200 students and 35 faculty, with more than 50 master's theses done. The model was envisioned, created, evaluated, and diffused effectively. It was a short-term (1995–2002) success.

There were four central roles for CEFP, one national and three local. At the national level, I served as project director, responsible for overall development and administration of the project. A national leadership group offered ongoing consultation, and an independent evaluator designed and implemented the external project evaluation with an evaluation advisory group.

Second, at the local level each of the 23 sites (22 regional offices and the NHO) identified a staff person to serve as evaluation facilitator. This role was to serve as the interface between ACS and the university and to lend necessary support to the faculty and student(s) who conducted studies. Further, the evaluation facilitator served as the primary contact for advisory group members. The evaluation advisory group of 8 to 10 people provided advice throughout the 6-to-9-month evaluation. Its primary role was to help the faculty advisor and evaluation fellow think through various program issues, review drafts of the evaluation plan and data collection instruments, offer insights into the collected data, and make recommendations based on the evaluation's findings.

Third, there was an identified faculty advisor at each participating university who had the responsibility for recruiting ACS evaluation fellows for one year using uniform criteria. Faculty members were paid a small stipend to supervise each evaluation fellow and to supply quality control for the study.

Fourth, the evaluation fellow(s) worked under the supervision of the faculty advisor and the evaluation facilitator, and with the project-specific evaluation advisory group to carry out an actual program evaluation of a local ACS program.

CEFP was an intentional ECB strategy to create an action system within ACS and its structure, culture, and everyday practices. Its purpose was to create and sustain spaces for professional expert program evaluation and its uses for program improvement and other decision making. Essential to managing ECB on the national and local levels were three orientations to the work. First, utilization-focused evaluation (UFE) was a framework for enhancing the utility and actual use of evaluations (Patton, 1997). Second, evaluation inquiry for learning in organizations (EILO) demonstrated to intended users the value of evaluation for learning and program improvement (Preskill & Torres, 1998). Third, Himmelman's model of collaboration for change (1994) offered a common definition of collaboration, its purpose, and how it could occur. The next section describes how each was operationalized in CEFP, and in so doing how managing ECB worked and whether it proved effective at ACS on the levels of studies and of organizational change in the short run (1995–2002) and the longer run (2003 to present).

For an overview of the CEFP, see Compton, Baizerman, Preskill, Rieker, and Miner (2001), a special supplement of *Cancer Practice* (Preskill & Compton, 2001), and a case study of CEFP as ECB (Compton et al., 2002). For the evaluation of CEFP, see Bonnet (1999, 2001).

Toward Conceptualizing ECB

Using the conceptual definition of ECB as a referent, this section describes how the overall managing of the ACS evaluation function was driven by a larger ECB vision described earlier in this article. ECB is defined conceptually by Stockdill, Baizerman, and Compton (2002, p. 8) as "a context-dependent, intentional action system of guided processes and practices for bringing about and sustaining a state of affairs in which quality program evaluation and its appropriate uses are ordinary and ongoing practices within and/or between one or more organizations/programs/sites." Three elements of ECB are described next, and examples are given from the ACS ECB effort to illustrate aspects of managing ECB.

Context-Dependent. The first element is being context-dependent, which means that whether and how ECB is carried out depends on the realities of each particular organization. The organizational structures, cultures, and processes at ACS were in some ways unique, as is likely true for any organization of some complexity and history.

ACS was a complex, formal, nationwide NGO with multiple layers (NHO, regional, and community-level offices), varying commitment to evaluation among them, and few staff trained to do professional program evaluation. At that time, the organization was undergoing major changes in its organization, resulting in a reduction from 50 state-level offices to 17 regional offices, and a downsizing of the national board of directors from several hundred members to fewer than 50. It was not clear to ACS's national leadership where to place the evaluation unit within the NHO structure, resulting in regular changes in its organizational location and thus my supervisor. ACS was then a self-referential organization, with no history of systematically soliciting and using feedback from program recipients or other external stakeholders, although it was a nationwide volunteer organization. The practice of evaluation as such was in conflict with many of the ways it understood, carried out, and promoted its work, and this contributed to tension surrounding the existence of the unit, the commitment of resources to its continuation, and whether evaluation staff were being invited "to the table" when program decisions were being made. In this organizational context, to build and sustain a viable evaluation unit meant that evaluation as such had to have a constituency advocating and supporting this work. CEFP was a strategy for building and sustaining this in ACS with its still-local offices, schools of public health university faculty, and renowned evaluation consultants from around the country.

Intentional Action System. The second element is an intentional action system, which means that ECB is done in an organization, program, or site by joining with others in ongoing collaboration and other forms of alliances and political relationships. Over time, there can arise sustained purposive systems. The ECB manager must be the agent who organizes, leads, and works to sustain development of action systems that advocate for and support evaluation. At ACS, the intentional action system included two components: CEFP and structures and processes for developing capacity and responding to requests from NHO staff for evaluation services.

The role of the ECB manager as co-creator of action systems has been shown in several ways; one was leading the development of a proposal to the Robert W. Woodruff Foundation to secure funding for CEFP. This yearlong process required building political alliances at the NHO and with the regional offices to garner support for the proposal, persistence in monitoring its progress, and ongoing conversation with ACS top leadership to ensure the proposal remained at the top of ACS's list of priorities for external funding.

Another example is found in the necessity to play multiple roles within ACS, among them evaluator, administrator, staff supervisor, funding entrepreneur, evaluation facilitator, and ECB manager, often all within one work day. This role repertoire included designing and implementing a study, managing a set of studies or a group of evaluators, as well as an organizational ECB structure and process across organizational levels and units, and maintaining regular communication among the ACS NHO and ACS regional offices and among ACS and the universities participating in the CEFP.

A third example was development of intraorganizational structures and processes that supported sustaining the new evaluation unit. This included securing ACS resources to support evaluation work, creating demand for the next study, and advocating for the use of all the studies. At the NHO, collaborative relationships were established with program management staff in other departments to implement and use evaluations. These were done primarily using independent consultants identified by the ECB manager, who compiled a roster of consultants as a way to build evaluation capacity and thus design, implement, and complete studies.

These three examples illustrate how the ECB manager worked bifocally, with one focus on the forest and the other simultaneously on the trees, developing and sustaining the overall ECB structure and process while designing and implementing specific, actual studies and their use. Development of intra- and interorganizational structures was an ongoing process managed both for the short run (completing discrete studies) and the longer run (developing and maintaining collaborative relationships and infrastructure to increase organizational capacity for evaluation). These were also used for everyday organizational work, such as finding funding.

Process. The definition includes another element, process. This refers to the overall intentional effort to create and sustain an ECB action system. Adoption of a highly process-oriented evaluation was a managerial stance. That is, regular and ongoing contact with key players (school of public health faculty, student fellows, independent consultants, ACS staff) was essential to ensuring that they felt they were part of this larger effort to bring evaluation to ACS, and more specifically a particular frame of evaluation and how to do it.

Foci could include developing and sustaining an evaluation unit, creating ongoing capacity to conduct evaluation studies, and working toward practical use of evaluation on the part of staff throughout the organization.

Most critical for developing and sustaining an organization's evaluation unit is the support of top leadership. At ACS, two ECB managers were crucial: the EVP, who made decisions on budget, new positions, staff promotions, and identification of topics to be evaluated; and me, the director of evaluation services, the midlevel ECB manager of the unit. This meant managing CEFP and external contractors, and working at the systematic organizational processes necessary to making evaluation a regular and routine part of all of ACS activities and decision making.

Central to the ACS ECB effort was a 15-step process for managing discrete evaluations. Designed and tested over a 5-year period at ACS, it was a way to operationalize Utilization-Focused Evaluation (Patton, 1997) and was central in two ways to the overall agency ECB strategy.

First, these steps were the process created to fashion a common understanding of evaluation at ACS, while also being the systematic way evaluation was to be designed, implemented, and used for program improvement and accountability. It was grounded in a participatory, collaborative model (Whitmore, 1998). It fit ACS's ethos as an organization of volunteers. ACS staff, volunteers, and contractors worked together doing and using each evaluation. This was made possible because the 15-step process clearly defined the roles of program manager (or designee) and evaluator (internal or external) as they worked with an evaluation study advisory group of primary intended users and stakeholders. It laid out a protocol for designing, implementing, and using the evaluation (Compton Glover-Kudon, Avery, & Morris, 2001). As intended, this became the taken-for-granted approach to ACS evaluation. As participants learned to work in this way, less support was needed from me at the central evaluation unit; new capacity to do and use evaluation was present on organizational levels from local to regional to national, and at CEFP sites nationwide. Another benefit of CEFP was that it created clear roles within the organization for doing and using evaluation. This too was an ECB benefit.

Managing Day-to-Day Activities and Managing for ECB

As the director of evaluation services, my work included two broad task orientations: everyday, ordinary, and mundane administrative duties and managing for ECB. The first set included developing and advocating within ACS for Evaluation Services budget, supervising ongoing evaluation studies, evaluation training for ACS staff, CEFP participants and volunteers, and the day-to-day managing of three professional evaluators and one support staff.

The everyday and mundane nature of this work—managing—must not lead to diminishing its crucial importance for evaluation. Rather, it is precisely these "ordinary," day-to-day activities that serve to make evaluation work possible. If this work is not done or if it is done poorly, then the unit can come to be seen as "functioning poorly" and become at risk of higher administrative control, budget reduction, a reduced mandate and field of operations, staff reductions, travel to the field curtailed, and the like. If managing the everyday is not done well, then it is difficult to manage for a second-order purpose, such as accountability, program improvement, or ECB.

Managing for ECB, as will be shown, is purposive work intended to change how an organization conceives of its evaluation work internally and externally. To manage for ECB is to go beyond managing an evaluation unit producing discrete studies, beyond managing a group of evaluators, and into managing systems and evaluators and studies in particular ways for particular purposes. To get at managing for ECB, we begin with a discussion of two broad, general orientations to managing evaluations: managing discrete studies (for accountability or program improvement) and then managing for ECB.

Managing Evaluation: Two Ideal Types

As discussed in Chapter 2, there is a surprisingly small amount of literature specific to managing evaluation, and little attention is given to models of managing appropriate for both evaluators and program managers who manage studies and ECB. On the basis of this literature and our own experiences, we discerned two major orientations, with related strategies: managing one or more specific studies and managing an evaluation capacity building system, that is, an ECB structure and process (Compton et al., 2002). Max Weber's ideal-type strategy is useful here to understand the two and the differences (Gerth & Mills, 1946). In this, a phenomenon is abstracted to some of its elements and traits. Some of them are amplified and others given less prominence so that in effect an abstraction is constructed and used heuristically to understand the phenomenon (here, the two managerial orientations). This strategy is not valuational in that it does not propose that one model is better than another or is perfect, which is to say, ideal.

Managing Discrete Studies. Program managers, evaluation managers, and evaluators work at managing structures and processes specific to one or more studies. Contracts for evaluators follow explicit project protocols about product, process, payment, and the like (Stufflebeam, 2008). Attention is on "getting the study done and used" in mutually beneficial ways (Bell, 2004). This includes the contractor's data needs, dates for draft and final reports ("products"), payment schedule, costs, and so on. Such managing is oriented to efficient, product-driven completion, in contrast to managing ECB.

Managing for ECB. The second ideal-type managerial orientation is to work at the structure and processes necessary for evaluation to become a regular and routine part of the organization's work, including regular use of study findings (Compton et al., 2002).

An ECB process challenges organizations to develop new ways of thinking about how to use evaluation and other empirical data in the routine practices of policy and program decision making. The ECB process emphasizes long-term infrastructure development and sustainability as one frame for short-term evaluation studies. To do ECB, someone must focus beyond the immediate study, beyond the process, completion, and timely use of a single evaluation study toward the multiple activities necessary for creating demand for evaluation as a regular and routine part of the organization's work. As a guiding principle, this person or group consistently questions what will be left after each discrete study is completed, and monitors increases in *sustainable evaluation structures and systems* as evidence of enhanced, necessary, and appropriate evaluation capacity.

ECB is never-ending; it is an ongoing, intentional effort to develop and sustain evaluation capacity (Compton et al., 2002). In this intent, ECB differs also from what most evaluation researchers are interested in and work at: single evaluation studies that meet the Joint Committee Standards (Joint Committee on Standards for Educational Evaluation, 1994) and client wants and needs. Typically, their goal is to improve programs, not to develop the necessary infrastructure and processes for sustaining evaluation and improving the *organization* sponsoring the program. This distinction is shown in Table 5.1, the managing orientation of the program evaluation manager and the ECB manager.

Principles of Managing ECB

As second-order, purposive work, day-to-day managing for ECB is built on the everyday activities of managing an evaluation group or unit within a formal organization (or in a postmodern network). What makes ECB different from managing evaluation for accountability or program improvement is the goal of institutionalizing the practice, thereby making it ordinary and mundane; ECB is a type of organizational change. Although it is too early in the history of ECB to have empirically based principles of practice, it is possible to suggest tentative principles from my work.

Principles for the practice of managing for ECB come from three sources: the intentionality of practice; the nature of ECB as such; and the manager's location and work in a formal organization, interorganizational system, or complex network.

Intentionality of the Practice. By definition, managing for ECB is intentional work, and this purpose must be explicit.

Because ECB is a complex practice, the ongoing structures and processes of managing ECB require an unusually high degree of continuous and empirical monitoring to ensure that the complex action system continues to be focused, appropriate, and effective.

Also because of its complexity, the manager must be especially self-reflexive and self-reflective to ensure that the everyday practice is intentional and purposive and fits the basic everyday administration of the unit.

Nature of ECB as Such. Managing for ECB is creating, sustaining, and managing explicit organizational structures and processes designed for the purposes of ECB. Managing for ECB should follow explicit guidelines

Table 5.1. Comparison of Managing Orientations to Evaluation Studies and to Evaluation Capacity Building

	Perspective	
	Program Evaluation Manager	Manager of ECB
Definition	Program evaluation is a process of systematically using a recognized evaluation model in accord with at least the Joint Committee's Standards to complete an agreed-upon program evaluation study in a timely way.	ECB is a context-dependent intentional action system of guided processes and practices for bringing about and sustaining a state of affairs in which quality program evaluation and its appropriate uses are ordinary and ongoing practices within or between one or more organizations, programs, and sites.
Actual practices	Doing quality program evaluations using acceptable models (for example, Stufflebeam and Shinkfield, 2007).	Ongoing guided processes and practices for bringing about and sustaining a state of affairs in which quality program evaluation and its appropriate uses are ordinary and ongoing practices within or between one or more organizations, programs, and sites.
Evaluator orientation	Evaluator does best science in carrying out a study and enhancing its likely uses.	Evaluator does best science in carrying out a study and enhancing its likely uses to make and keep evaluation a necessary, everyday part of an organization's structure, culture, and work practices internally and in relation to other entities in its environment.
Manager orientation	Manager may be the evaluator or someone else who has the responsibility to make the best science-based study happen.	Manager tries to support ongoing evaluation function by creating the necessary structures and processes so that any manager in the organization could learn enough about evaluation to facilitate an evaluation study, find an appropriate evaluator, and integrate evaluation into the ongoing program improvement process and for accountability.
Sample manager activities	Supports evaluator by: • Identifying necessary resources for evaluation • Solving problems so the evaluator can do the work • Developing collaborative relationships to support use of evaluation • Developing practical policies for contracting studies (e.g., cost, timeline)	Supports organizational development by: • Creating a common understanding of evaluation within the organization • Creating standard processes so that quality evaluation is done and used • Developing and sustaining collaborative relationships to support short- and long-term organizational development by using evaluation • Works to ensure an ongoing demand for evaluation and its uses

such as those in Compton, Baizerman, and Stockdill (2002) of overall process, actual practices, and occupational orientation. Managing for ECB is a value-based orientation (that is, it is a good that organizations have institutionalized evaluation), and the set of core values includes co-creating and co-sustaining as ways of working with stakeholders and intended users, whether inside or outside the organization. ECB is never finished; managing for ECB is never finished.

Manager's Location and Work in a Formal Organization, Interorganizational System, or Complex Network. In a postmodern organizational environment of complex networks, managing for ECB is more complex, requiring richer cognitive maps, different administrative and political skills, and new types of timing of action and the like. By definition, managing for ECB is political work in the sense of ongoing negotiations with colleagues over power, authority, resources, responsibility, and the rest, and it must be recognized and carried out as such.

What Remains?

By 2008, what remains of the system and activities begun at ACS? First, the ACS Evaluation Institute became a collaborative effort between ACS and CDC, then a CDC event, and now a CDC/AEA annual summer institute. Second, ECB has become a topic of practice and scholarship. Last, many of the ACS evaluation fellows are now working, some after having obtained an advanced degree, in public health evaluation.

Acknowledgments

I would like to thank Lei Zhang and William Winans for their editorial support in preparing this article, and Bruce Black for his review of the text and help in updating American Cancer Society information.

References

Bell, J. B. (2004). Managing evaluation projects. In J. S. Wholey, H. P. Hatry, & K. Newcomer (Eds.), *Handbook of practical program evaluation* (2nd ed.). San Francisco: Jossey-Bass.

Bonnet, D. (1999). *An evaluation of year one of the American Cancer Society's Collaborative Evaluation Fellows Project.* Indianapolis, IN: D. Bonnet and Associates.

Bonnet, D. (2001). An external evaluator's perspective on the CEFP. *Cancer Practice,* (Suppl. 1), S72–S77.

Compton, D., Baizerman, M., & Stockdill, S. H. (Eds.). (2002). *The art, craft, and science of Evaluation Capacity Building. New Directions for Evaluation, 93.*

Compton, D., Baizerman, M., Preskill, H., Rieker, P., & Miner, K. (2001). Developing evaluation capacity while improving evaluation training in public health: The American Cancer Society's Collaborative Evaluation Fellows Project. *Evaluation and Program Planning, 24,* 33–40.

Compton, D., Glover-Kudon, R., Avery E., & Morris C. (2001). The Collaborative Evaluation Fellows Project: Background and overview of the model. *Cancer Practice, 9* (Suppl.1), S4–S10.

Compton, D., Glover-Kudon, R., Smith, I., & Avery, E. (2002). Ongoing capacity building in the American Cancer Society (ACS) 1995–2001. In D. Compton, M. Baizerman, & S. H. Stockdill (Eds.), *The art, craft, and science of Evaluation Capacity Building. New Directions for Evaluation, 93,* 47–61.

Gerth, H., & Mills, C. (Eds.). (1946). From Max Weber: *Essays in sociology.* New York: Oxford University Press.

Himmelman, A. (1994). Collaboration for a change: Definitions, models, roles, and a guide for collaborative processes. In M. Herman (Ed.), *Resolving conflict: Strategies for local government.* Washington, DC: International City/County Management Association.

Joint Committee on Standards for Educational Evaluation. (1994). *The program evaluation standards.* Thousand Oaks, CA: Sage.

Patton, M. Q. (1997). *Utilization-Focused Evaluation: The new century text* (3rd ed.). Thousand Oaks, CA: Sage.

Preskill, H., & Compton, D. (Eds.). (2001). The American Cancer Society's Collaborative Evaluation Fellows Project: A nationwide program evaluation strategy. *Cancer Practice, 9* (Suppl. 1).

Preskill, H., & Torres, R. T. (1998). *Evaluative inquiry for learning in organizations.* Thousand Oaks, CA: Sage.

Stockdill, S. H., Baizerman, M., & Compton, D. W. (2002). Toward a definition of the ECB process: A conversation with the ECB literature. In D.W. Compton, M. Baizerman, & S. H. Stockdill (Eds.), *The art, craft, and science of evaluation capacity building. New Directions for Evaluation, 93,* 7–25.

Stufflebeam, D. L. (2008). *Evaluation contracts checklist.* Retrieved September 10, 2008, from http://www.wmich.edu/evalctr/checklists

Stufflebeam, D. L., & Shinkfield, A. J. (2007). *Evaluation theory, models, and applications.* San Francisco: Jossey-Bass.

Whitmore, E. (Ed.). (1998). *Understanding and practicing participatory evaluation. New Directions for Evaluation, 80.*

DONALD W. COMPTON is former director of evaluation services, National Home Office, American Cancer Society; and adjunct faculty, Emory University, Rollins School of Public Health. He is the corresponding editor for this issue and is reachable at donaldcompton03@comcast.net.

NEW DIRECTIONS FOR EVALUATION • DOI: 10.1002/ev

Schooley, M. W. (2009). Managing evaluation in a federal public health setting. In D. W. Compton & M. Baizerman (Eds.), *Managing program evaluation: Towards explicating a professional practice*. New Directions for Evaluation, 121, 71–78.

6

Managing Evaluation in a Federal Public Health Setting

Michael W. Schooley

Abstract

The author, a federal manager who leads development and maintenance of evaluation for specific public health programs at the Centers for Disease Control and Prevention, tells the story of developing an evaluation unit in the Office on Smoking and Health. Lessons about managing evaluation, including his practices and related principles, are presented. © Wiley Periodicals, Inc.*

Over the past 10 years, I have endeavored to build and sustain the acceptance and practice of program evaluation. I have tried to establish program evaluation as a regular, ongoing strategy for accountability and improvement of federal disease prevention and control programs. Here I share the lessons learned and the practical strategies employed with others facing similar challenges and opportunities.

Note: The views and opinions expressed in this article are those of the author and do not necessarily represent the views of the Centers for Disease Control and Prevention.

NEW DIRECTIONS FOR EVALUATION, no. 121, Spring 2009   © Wiley Periodicals, Inc., and the American Evaluation Association. * This article is a US Government work and, as such, is in the public domain in the United States of America.   Published online in Wiley InterScience (www.interscience.wiley.com) • DOI: 10.1002/ev.286

71

I began practicing evaluation and surveillance at the Centers for Disease Control and Prevention (CDC) in 1993. In 1998, I started building and managing an evaluation and surveillance unit at CDC's Office on Smoking and Health (OSH). I expanded my experience by practicing and managing evaluation activities aimed at prevention and control of obesity, as well as heart disease and stroke. Today, I manage the Applied Research and Evaluation Branch in the Division for Heart Disease and Stroke Prevention. I attained these responsibilities with little formal training in program evaluation or management. I was opportunistic about meeting a demonstrated need for evaluation, and I developed the knowledge, skills, and resources to succeed. I offer my practical knowledge from building and managing evaluation capacity and competency in a federal agency.

Building, Sustaining, and Managing Evaluation

In 1993, I began working with OSH to conduct surveillance studies describing the burden of tobacco on society and to inform the planning and monitoring of national and state-level public health programs. CDC allocates funding and support to state health departments for tobacco prevention and control programs. By 1997, state settlements with the tobacco industry had become an imminent reality that would directly affect public health practice. One of the first state settlements occurred in Florida, and it led to a 2-year pilot program of more than $100 million to address tobacco use among youth (USD-HHS, 2000). Florida and other states turned to CDC for guidance and technical assistance to help plan, implement, and evaluate tobacco prevention and control programs.

A small team within OSH was pulled together to furnish technical assistance and guidance to states. The team included experts in the areas of health promotion and disease prevention programs, health communications, surveillance, research, and evaluation. As a relatively junior staff member, I was honored to be among the core group of consultants who worked closely with several state health department colleagues to develop these programs. During this actual practice, I learned about program evaluation and began to think in those terms.

Recognizing and Adapting to the Environment. When I joined OSH, I never heard anyone say, "I noticed that there is no evaluation capacity here; let's think about developing some." Instead, pressure from outside of CDC was our motivating force, inviting us to step up and develop evaluation capacity. This external pressure from the states was the impetus that prompted us to start program evaluation practices.

In OSH, we started looking for opportunities to build a team to respond to states' need for evaluation. One of the first things we recognized was the importance of linking evaluation to tobacco use surveillance, which offers a wealth of data relevant to evaluation questions. This connection between evaluation and surveillance is especially important in the organizational

NEW DIRECTIONS FOR EVALUATION • DOI: 10.1002/ev

context of CDC, where surveillance is an essential public health tool for policymakers and program developers. Thus we did not try to establish evaluation as an entirely new strategy. Instead, we tied evaluation to something that we already knew how to do well. Surveillance was a core and valued public health strategy at CDC and we linked evaluation directly to it. By developing the two together, it became easier for others in CDC and the states to notice, accept, and support evaluation.

Because of limited staffing and resources within OSH, building the evaluation team required that we identify where to obtain existing or low-cost resources to invest in the team. Recognizing that civil service positions would take more time to secure, we built the team through formal federal fellowship programs, such as the Presidential Management Fellows Program. In addition, we used other fellowship programs to identify and interview young professionals who showed interest and enthusiasm for evaluation. Those few of us in OSH who were working on evaluation mentored the junior staff. A few years later, we secured civil service positions to formalize and sustain the team.

We developed evaluation capacity by taking on intramural projects. We focused more on developing intramural personnel and staff capacity, and less on stretching scarce resources to build a portfolio of funded extramural projects. For instance, we recognized that it would be easier to get $50,000 for a fellow position than to get much more to support extramurally contracted activities; thus we were able to successfully start building evaluation capacity.

Sustaining and further developing our evaluation capacity relied on being product-oriented. Constituents and decision makers consider products a measure of success. When a team develops and effectively promotes useful products or major events, their value to the organization increases. It is crucial to complete the work (product) and actively promote and disseminate it to various constituents. We spent as much time disseminating and promoting our work as we did completing it. Our products and a general awareness of our work generated much interest and value in our team. Therefore, decision makers were willing to invest more resources and effort into building, sustaining, and developing our team.

Being action- and product-oriented and responsive helped to build and sustain the team and staff. The team grew from two to 20 staff in approximately 4 years. To support this growth, we developed a vision for evaluation. When an opportunity arose to request staff and budget, we had a plan to put in front of leadership to move evaluation forward and use resources effectively.

The mission of the evaluation and surveillance team was to collaborate with state health departments by extending support, guidance, and technical assistance. Although collaboration has a long history in health education and more recently has been expressed in principles of participatory research, it is still uncommon among many traditionally trained scientists and researchers. Completing our mission through the successful practice of surveillance and evaluation requires diverse sets of skills and types of people. The surveillance and research that was our core work was very detail-oriented, deductive, and founded on well-established methods. On the other hand, evaluation can be more inductive, often with less-established approaches, and ad hoc or emergent in its use of strategy and tools. For instance, surveillance requires comfort with data management, analysis, statistics, and methods. Program evaluation requires comfort with synthesizing information quickly, making decisions, and moving forward in several directions, often without enough information, clear standards, or guidelines. Therefore, to build the evaluation and surveillance team we had to find the right mixture of skills and qualities in our staff. As a result, the team was multidisciplinary and could practice evaluation and surveillance with many CDC constituents.

As the team developed, groups formed on the basis of dissimilar professional orientations: those who worked on surveillance and those who worked on evaluation. The link between surveillance and evaluation was evident, but there was little opportunity for cross-fertilization of skills. Moreover, we could not function effectively by assigning staff from surveillance and evaluation to each project because of the rising demand for service and resource constraints. Additionally, team members were using the majority of their time to supply consultation and technical assistance and little time to conduct their own surveillance and evaluation studies. For professionals who come to CDC for the public health science of surveillance or evaluation, spending the majority of their time on technical assistance calls is not ideal. The 6 hours each day on the phone giving technical assistance offered a somewhat intangible and less recognizable benefit to leadership, whereas 6 hours a day conducting a study and publishing information offered a more tangible and familiar result and benefit to leadership.

To address these challenges, I began to reorganize the team and remove separate evaluation and surveillance groups. In addition, the reorganization was intended to equalize and reduce the consultation burden across all team members. Team members were given the opportunity to expand their skills with each having responsibilities in evaluation and surveillance. This change gave team members a better sense of how surveillance and evaluation complemented each other, but it proved to be an unsustainable model. Some of the surveillance activities that require depth of knowledge and attention to detail started to suffer, and the quality of our research started to decline. The requirements were too diverse for staff to meet the range of expectations and demands placed on them. In hindsight, it was a good strategy to ensure that people had an understanding and respect for what others were doing. Although this strategy may be practical in the short run for cross-training, it was not sustainable in the long run because demands for quality work were high and persistent. Therefore, we reorganized again and went back to adaptation of the earlier model.

I realized that sustaining and managing an evaluation team required a different approach from the effort to initially develop the team. It's important to continuously reinvent the team and work to fit the changing context and dynamics of a group.

Gaining Perspectives. As an evaluation and surveillance team lead, I was working on program evaluation from a scientific perspective, applied and grounded in state programs and practices. I had little experience with evaluation from a higher-level perspective or as viewed by the Office of Management and Budget (OMB) and Government Accounting Office (GAO). In 2002, I had the opportunity to see my work from another perspective when I took a temporary assignment as OSH associate director for policy, planning, and coordination. Through this experience, I acquired greater appreciation for the balance among evaluation that examines program effectiveness, evaluation that serves program improvement, and evaluation to meet the demands of accountability. As a result, I could distinguish between the purposes and approaches and how an evaluation unit can address a range of evaluation issues.

Managing Evaluation

Michael Wargo (1983) wrote in an earlier volume of *New Directions for Evaluation* about the complexities of the federal system and the resultant difficulties in managing programs, staff, and budget. I experienced similar challenges in the day-to-day management of evaluation studies and units. To overcome the challenges and develop a valued and credible evaluation unit, my practice and management principles are to:

- Be action-oriented
- Be responsive
- Be product-oriented
- Develop perspective, knowledge, and competence

Being Action-Oriented. Being action-oriented includes readiness to act and a proactive posture. I try always to be ready to act—to be organized and opportunistic when seizing a possibility to move an evaluation project and team forward. In addition, I try to be proactive—to plan ahead and have a vision to strengthen and develop an evaluation team's size, scope, and depth. I develop and keep plans ready for potential staffing, projects, and products so that I can respond quickly and substantively. For example, if a staff position opens up unexpectedly, I have a plan for this position to support existing work and advance work in other important areas. In the federal system, resources can become available, and it can be challenging to identify viable funding mechanisms quickly. Being prepared and committed to act presents the opportunity to advance important work under these circumstances.

Being proactive and ready to act means using formal and informal organizational systems, including contacting long-time colleagues throughout the agency to monitor and watch for opportunities to advance the work of the evaluation team. It is important to learn these systems and related organizational cultures to understand better how they can support team development and sustainability.

Being Responsive. Responsiveness relates directly to the first principle, being action-oriented. I try to be fully responsive to my staff, our constituents, managers, and administrators. I deliver what is requested promptly and substantively. I anticipate who may ask for something and when they might ask, and I am flexible and strive to prioritize requests appropriately. After many years at CDC, I have a sense of when to expect the unexpected and how to respond accordingly.

To be responsive I need to know the system I work within, as well as the people with whom I work. Responsiveness includes quickly assessing requests, what and why I am being asked, how my response will be used, and by whom. I need to know my staff and their work to quickly assess my needs and who can help to address them. In addition, I try to identify how quickly to respond (that is, how much of a priority is the "emergency"? How long is it likely to last? What is the anticipated result if I am slow to respond?). Moreover, I need to know the organizational structure and culture, schedules, political nature, meanings, and people in order to create an understanding of how my work environment operates.

Being Product-Oriented. I always manage people, projects, and budgets with a focus on production. I try to structure our work to generate products quickly for our constituents, among them CDC, state health departments, the U.S. Department of Health and Human Services, Congress, the academic community, professional groups, and citizens. In my experience, products are tangible benefits that various constituents can see and assess. In turn, products help constituents recognize the value of a work unit. Because some products are intangible, I try to think about how knowledge gained from an evaluation can become a tangible and valuable product. I am especially proud of several products from groups I managed. Among them are Introduction to Program Evaluation; Surveillance and Evaluation Data Resources; Key Outcome Indicators; the STATE System; and the Division for Heart Disease and Stroke Prevention Evaluation Plan (MacDonald et al., 2001; Yee and Schooley, 2001; Starr et al., 2005; CDC, 2008).

Develop Perspective, Knowledge, and Competence. In addition to the three principles, it is important to constantly develop perspective, knowledge, and competence in evaluation and management. I presented examples of these principles and shared my experience building, managing, and sustaining evaluation in a federal government context. In my experience, context plays an important role when applying these principles. Here are a few additional lessons related to context:

- Recognize how the work environment and social values shape evaluation practice and management in a given context.

NEW DIRECTIONS FOR EVALUATION • DOI: 10.1002/ev

- Adapt evaluation to the work context, recognizing how it differs from other essential research strategies and understanding how stakeholders and clients view it as a service.
- Adopt different perspectives on evaluation practice and management to enhance both.

How I Manage

Until I was invited to write about my experience, I did not spend much time reflecting on my management practice. The editors of this issue asked me to articulate my practice principles and the approach I use to guide and assess my own work and the work of others. In addition to the principles and lessons I discussed previously, within my group I keep abreast of the progress of evaluation projects, the project timelines, and when results and products will be available. I strive to begin sharing the information quickly and, hopefully, start to influence evaluation practice and inform and inspire future work. I always keep the end products in mind. I try to be aware of where things fit, where they could go, and where opportunities could be seized to move something forward.

Additional skills and techniques that I use include listening to my colleagues and fostering opportunities to bring people and projects together. I try to see how items can be combined and transformed into something more useful and more than the sum of the individual items. As described earlier, linking surveillance and evaluation helped to strengthen and advance both areas. In addition, I work to identify issues as they emerge, before they have been fully formed, and to seize the opportunity to shape the situation through attentiveness to evaluation projects and the environmental context.

Day-to-day management involves managing on the edge of what something could become and looking for opportunities to turn possibility into action. I work to build and sustain demand for evaluation, to respond to this demand, and to rebuild the demand for evaluation again, ad infinitum.

Acknowledgments

I acknowledge and thank the various CDC supervisors and leaders for whom I have worked and those who have recognized and supported evaluation practice, especially Janet Collins, Rosemarie Henson, and Darwin Labarthe.

References

Centers for Disease Control and Prevention. (2008). *Division evaluation plan*. Atlanta, GA: Division for Heart Disease and Stroke Prevention, CDC.
Centers for Disease Control and Prevention. *State tobacco activities tracking and evaluation (STATE) system*. Retrieved July 25, 2008, from http://www.cdc.gov/tobacco/statesystem

MacDonald, G., Starr, G., Schooley, M., Yee, S. L., Klimowski, K., & Turner, K. (2001). *Introduction to program evaluation for comprehensive tobacco control programs.* Atlanta, GA: Centers for Disease Control and Prevention, CDC.

Starr, G., Rogers, T., Schooley, M., Porter, S., Wiesen, E., & Jamison, N. (2005). *Key outcome indicators for evaluating comprehensive tobacco control programs.* Atlanta, GA: Centers for Disease Control and Prevention, CDC.

U.S. Department of Health and Human Services, Centers for Disease Control and Prevention, National Center for Chronic Disease Prevention and Health Promotion. (2000). *Reducing tobacco use: A report of the surgeon general.* Atlanta, GA: Author.

Wargo, M. J. (1983). Management of the evaluation function within the federal government. In R. G. St. Pierre (Ed.), *Management and organization of program evaluation. New Directions for Program Evaluation, 18.*

MICHAEL W. SCHOOLEY is chief of the Applied Research and Evaluation Branch, Division for Heart Disease and Stroke Prevention, Centers for Disease Control and Prevention.

NEW DIRECTIONS FOR EVALUATION • DOI: 10.1002/ev

Baizerman, M., & Compton, D. W. (2009). What did we learn from the case studies about managing evaluation? In D. W. Compton & M. Baizerman (Eds.), *Managing program evaluation: Towards explicating a professional practice. New Directions for Evaluation, 121,* 79–86.

7

What Did We Learn From the Case Studies About Managing Evaluation?

Michael Baizerman, Donald W. Compton

Abstract

Case studies about managing evaluation are examined for perspectives on expertise in managing evaluation. There are lessons on a geography of managing, managing as organizational work, the notions of "competency" and "expertise," and managing evaluation as professional work. Dreyfus and Dreyfus (2004) offer a framework for an introductory discussion of the essentials of expertise, as does Ryle's distinction (1949) between "knowing that" (about) and "knowing how" (to). © Wiley Periodicals, Inc.

One approach to analyzing case materials is to interrogate them to learn about the practice of managing evaluation; this we do first. A second approach is to use the cases to answer some of the basic questions in Chapter 1. Here we move to deepen the understanding of managing evaluation. This prepares the ground for enriching an exploration of expertise in managing evaluation.

To begin, we restate our practical definition of effective managing of evaluation. The phrase *effective managing of evaluation* means the practical, everyday, professional expertise necessary to bring about the implementation and use of quality studies, the development of productive workers, and the sustaining of a well-run, ongoing, and influential evaluation unit.

What do the case data tell about the expertise of managing evaluation? Begin with practical everyday expertise. First, what do the case data tell us that we already know from the literature in our field and from practice experience? Most basic are these: Expertise is in part "knowing already," that is, knowing what to expect; it is simultaneity and juggling—having to do "a million things at once." It is having "a good clutch," which means constantly and quickly shifting gears from one demand to another, again and again over the work day. To work in this way requires particular expertise and good staff whom one trusts. It also requires standardization.

Second, what do the case data tell us about evaluation managing as professional work? The studies show, possibly because of sample bias, that basic managing expertise lies in "already knowing," that is, in "knowing about" and "knowing how to" (do) evaluation studies (as an evaluator), and knowing what is likely to be asked for, requested, and demanded by whom, when, and in what form(s). Managing evaluation is professional work grounded in evaluation studies, but essentially it is about how to do organization work.

The cases show that the core practice of managing evaluation is tridirectional (up, down, and across) and trilevel (studies, workers, and organizational unit). Put these together with the purpose of the evaluation unit and the purpose of specific evaluation studies, and the resulting matrix maps much of the space of the geography of managing (Figure 7.1). Using this matrix, one finds that the case studies suggest that the unit's purpose (organizational location, resources, and so on) frames the purpose of individual studies (internal to and external from the organization), with differences in managing seen in relations with clients (across and above) and activities, such as possibly more emphasis on explaining study purpose and findings when the unit is focused on accountability or program improvement, in contrast to ECB-focused. Basic to managing for all three purposes, for example,

Figure 7.1. The Geography of Managing

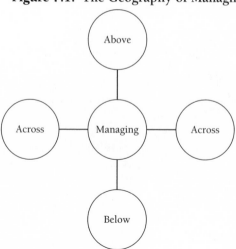

is advocating and defending the unit within and outside one's organization. Basic expertise is knowing already what and how to do what must be done on these three levels and in all three directions.

Expertise is:

- Above—to one's own boss(es)
- Across—to other units within and outside one's organization
- Below—to one's own workers

Work is trilevel:

- *Studies*—build demand; do studies; use studies
- *Workers*—supervise and develop workers as workers
- *Unit*—build demand for evaluation and for unit; sustain unit by doing its everyday work

Management and Managing Is Organization Work

Managing is organizational practice. "*Manager*" is a structural organizational position. Evaluations can be of programs, activities, interventions, or policies.

Managing is an organizational practice in that it takes place within this context and is bound in its particulars in large part by how each organization works—its form and practices, its structure and social norms, its culture, meanings, procedures and "ways" (Alvesson, 1993; Schultz, 1994). To talk about managing is to bring along this organizational context, which comes as foreground, middle ground, and background, as time and place, as what is to be done and as "how things are done around here." *Managing thus is always the managing-in-organizational-context* of evaluation studies, evaluators and other workers, and an evaluation unit.

Organizationally located, the manager is a structural position and space, and this tells us in organizational structural terms who the manager is related to, that is, who is above, below, and to the sides in the organization's written and actual structures. When organizational structure is read as "how things work around here," this tells us who supervises or manages the manager and who the manager supervises or manages. In practice, things may not be as clear as this, but our emphasis on organizational structure is intended to locate both this type of work and how it is positionally organized, and to prevent any reductionism, which tries to explain the work and how it is done while excluding the organization as base and context. We hope also to prevent other determinisms arguing that the work is as it is because (it is caused by) organizational position; this reification we reject also.

The manager has a "manager job." How the individual understands and carries this out depends in good part on the organization and its realities, and also on the individual and his or her membership in a practice community (Wenger, 1998) and its ethos and expertise.

Elements of the Expertise of Managing Evaluation

The case studies show expertise in managing. How is this expertise to be understood? Note the phrase; we did not write the "expertise of the manager," or "managerial expertise." Our focus is expertise in the doing of managing. Stevahn, King, Ghere, and Minnema (2005) use "competency" as their approach, while others move from "skill" (Ericsson, Charness, Feltovich, & Hoffman, 2006) to "expertise" (Dreyfus & Dreyfus, 1988, 2005). Sennett (2008) reminds us of Polanyi's "tact knowledge"—"we know more than we can tell," a form of knowing how to. There is "recipe knowledge" (Shaffer and Shaffer, 2006), rules of thumb, "practice wisdom" (O'Sullivan, 2005; Sheppard, 1995), "mother's wit," common sense, know-how (Hager, 2002), folk wisdom, and cookbook knowledge. All of these types of practical, everyday knowledge matter, along with scientific knowledge. In this historical moment, evidence-based practice is hegemonic, a philosophy (and ideology and politics) guiding applied professional practice, such as the everyday managing of evaluation. This is the knowledge of "applied science."

To follow Dreyfus and Dreyfus (2005), expertise "is based on the making of immediate, unreflective, situational responses; intuitive judgment is the hallmark of expertise" (p. 789). Here we want to sensitize the reader to the obvious but too easily forgotten point that there are many ways to get at understanding expertise in managing, and to categorize this expertise in two forms: "knowing that, what, and about" and "knowing how to" (Ryle, 1949). (See Ericsson et al., 2006.)

To the master managers in the case studies, much of what they do they already know. That is, they have long experience doing the work and cannot easily name and analyze their practice. They experience themselves as expert in doing what they do, expressing their "highest talent to its fullest measure," what Aristotle called excellence, and what Dreyfus and Dreyfus (2005) call expertise, the highest level in their five-stage model.

In the case studies, their expertise shows itself in the "already known," "done that before," "know how to do this." They have set up systems, procedures, rules, and practices that institutionalized the work so there is a standard way to do it, albeit one that is flexible and responsive to situation, context, politics, and personality. More than anything, they are systematic and in this way, using their standardized templates, they are able to effectively respond to the never-ending demands from above, below, and alongside them; this is how they work to order or control the omnipresence and simultaneity of the demands characterizing their everyday work world; there is always something, and usually many somethings at once.

In more typical terms, their expertise is in knowing which systems to set up, modify, sustain, and defend (to get the work done), and in knowing whom they need to do this. Systems and people in place, their expertise is seen as managing workflow, the worker-research-study nexus in time. They are and see themselves as jugglers, even when their workplace is to them not quite a circus! This point is well caught in the phrase "obedience to the moment has primacy," a phrase used to discuss the African American improvisational jazz aesthetic. The work is improvisational, within more or less normative, situational practices (Hadju, 2008).

The case study masters use standard, everyday management terms when they tell us what they do, how, and why. For example, in Chapter 4 Rodosky and Muñoz note that "because of my project management experience, I budget the cost of processes associated with the work, including data acquisition, input, storage, analysis, and reporting." They also describe their organizational structure in everyday management terms as follows:

> The basic structure of the Accountability, Research, and Planning Department is organized around outcomes. Our bottom line is customer service focused on student learning. The department's delivery system operates on well-defined objectives organized within a framework that is both vertically and horizontally aligned. The vertical alignment comes directly from our superintendent; the chain of command from him to my staff and me is clearly established and concerned with the flow of authority and responsibility. Horizontal alignment arises from my knowing the strengths and weaknesses of my departmental team.

In one sense, this usage deceives, hiding their expertise—their knowing what and how to, in conventional language. It is precisely the *rightness of their knowing,* its accuracy and validity, wherein lives their mastery. Typical of expert practitioners, they have so deeply and well integrated their knowing that it is typically unavailable to them to name, as Dreyfus and Dreyfus (2005) recognize.

Less obvious in their case study writing, but clear in person, is the authors' confidence in their knowledge and judgment, even when unsure about a specific situation or problem. Their feet are on solid ground, they know they are good at managing, they are experienced, and they accept this as their expertise and as (part of) their professional identity.

Is any of this unusual compared to managing social science research, other research, other activities, or a restaurant? Not really. What differences there are have to do with particulars: the nature of the evaluation enterprise; its particular knowledge workers; and the type, size, resources, and location of the evaluation unit. Quite important is the preferred community of practice in which they claim membership: Most but not all belong to the American Evaluation Association (AEA) and attend annual meetings, read the journals, and so on. All follow AEA practice guidelines.

This discussion is another step in understanding what managing is, how it works, and how its expertise shows itself (and how expert managers practice). It adds data for the decision by the evaluation profession and its organizations on the policy questions of whether or not to recognize managing as a basic expertise in evaluation practice; whether or not to educate and train this expertise; and whether or not trained, professional evaluators are better suited than those not trained in evaluation to manage evaluation studies, workers, and an evaluation unit. The central notion in our understanding of managing is expertise.

Doing Expertise and Telling How It Was Done

The master managers in these case studies show their expertise, their mastery, in its doing, in its practice, in *how* they do their work. They are merely more or less competent in *telling* how they do their expertise. When invited and then pushed to do so, they easily retreat to their training and talk in that language and from that perspective. This is a known feature of expertise (Dreyfus & Dreyfus, 2005; Schön, 1983).

The masters do show, demonstrate, and accomplish their expertise; they coach, mentor, tutor, guide, and advise their workers and student interns on evaluation research practice. They do the same on matters about the organization unit in relation to other units within their own organization and to those other agencies and programs. In these consultations and technical assistance, seen again is their managing expertise, and in these instances it is more explicit. In these instances of expertise showing itself are found the types of knowing called practice wisdom, rules of thumb, recipe knowledge, and otherwise.

It is known to be easier to get at the "what" of knowing, the "knowing that," the cognitive, than to get at the "how of doing," the "knowing how to." A fine recent book is *How Doctors Think* (Groopman, 2007). What physicians do is mostly observable; how they do this is far less obvious. This is true too for nursing (Benner, Tanner, & Chelsa, 1996) and other crafts (Sennett, 2008) and professions. This is true for managing as well; the closer in to the actual act, the more expertise as an integrative praxis shows itself as a whole, as "expertise." So too with skill as such. Much literature shows the scholarly effort to analytically and experimentally get at the constitutive elements of skill (Ericsson et al., 2006) across a variety of expertise, from chess mastery to hitting a baseball.

Managing is difficult to do and seemingly difficult for practitioners to describe, analyze, and teach, except by example. What is needed is a vocabulary and skill in its use. Until then, being mentored seems to be the best way for a novice to grasp managing as ordinary, mundane professional work.

At the end of the day, quality managing is done, expertise shows itself, and some practitioners move from novice to expert managing; they know what to do, when, and how, at a high level of skill, and are consistent and effective. It remains to be fully understood how all of this works. Empirical studies would help, and these would likely follow if the profession gave attention to this topic.

If managing expertise is not yet clear, managing evaluation as professional work is.

Managing Evaluation as Professional Work

The case studies show clearly that managing is a form of expertise. When managing is by professional evaluators, it is a different practice than when it is done by professionals trained and experienced in other fields. Expertise lies in part in already knowing what is likely to come up in doing research, with workers, and in the organization unit and beyond.

Evaluators who are professionally educated, especially those experienced doing evaluation studies, typically understand themselves as members of a practice community of evaluators (Wenger, 1998),that is, as professional evaluators. In their education they come to understand and accept the field's understanding of itself, its ethos, and its way of making sense of and doing scientific evaluation work. As elements in this professional socialization are its craft orientation to the work (Bensman & Lilienfeld, 1973), its stance toward the work and toward the world beyond itself and its gaze—how the world is seen, ordered, interpreted, and responded to. A professional evaluator sees oneself in all of this, as a part of this and for this to be a part of who one is, one's professional identity, and to be seen by others in this way (meaning, as an evaluator, an evaluation professional).

Every actual evaluator brings himself or herself as evaluator professional to the organizational position. What he does is who he is as an evaluator; who he is as an evaluator is, if he is fortunate, what he does at work. Who she is and what she does is also shaped by how she reads the world and acts within it. How she does the work is as evaluator. If he is always evaluator, he is also to himself sometimes a manager. To the observing world, he or she is always simultaneously both evaluator and manager.

As manager, he holds an organizational position which sets terms for how he will manage studies, workers, and the unit. If he does not have specialized training in managing, his primary professional identity may continue to be that of evaluator, and his job identity may be manager, evaluator or, somehow, both. If the evaluator does have specialized training and great experience in managing, she again may hold both identities, moving from one to another as situationally appropriate. Surely the case examples in this issue exemplify this. The primary orientation as manager is to facilitate studies, manage evaluators and others, and run the unit the way units are run in that organization and in the best way to make quality evaluation useful. Managing evaluators, she will likely use both her grounding in evaluation research and in supervision, human relations and personnel, also drawing on them to manage the unit.

Conclusion

Managing evaluation is a practice largely invisible in the professional literature, excepting when it is about managing studies. It is mundane work, and this in part contributes to its not being noticed. Often it is behind the scenes work and thus out of sight and in turn generally beyond research and training. Yet this chapter has begun to show that the practice and expertise of managing evaluation can be located, illuminated, and named; it is neither invisible nor ineffable. We next deepen and enrich this beginning grasp and understanding with more far-ranging explorations of several topics, including managing as lived practice and *phronesis*, in the traditions of *techné* and *episteme*.

References

Alvesson, M. (1993). *Cultural perspectives on organizations*. Cambridge, England: Cambridge University Press.

Benner, P., Tanner, C. A., & Chelsa, C. A. (1996). *Expertise in nursing practice: Caring, clinical judgment, and ethics*. New York: Springer.

Bensman, J., & Lilienfeld, R. (1973). *Craft and consciousness: Occupational technique and the development of world images*. New York: Wiley.

Dreyfus, H. L., & Dreyfus, S. E. (1988). *Mind over machine*. New York: Free Press.

Dreyfus, H. L., & Dreyfus, S. E. (2004). The ethical implications of five-stage skill acquisition model. *Bulletin of Science, Technology, and Society, 24*(3), 251–264.

Dreyfus, H. L., & Dreyfus, S. E. (2005). Peripheral vision: Expertise in real world contexts. *Organization Studies, 26*(5), 779–792.

Ericsson, K. A., Charness, N., Feltovich, P. J., & Hoffman, R. R. (Eds.). (2006). *The Cambridge handbook of expertise and expert performance*. Cambridge, England: Cambridge University Press.

Groopman, J. (2007). *How doctors think*. Boston: Houghton Mifflin.

Hadju, D. (2008, February 24). JazzMan. New York Times Book Review. *New York Times*, p. 25.

Hager, P. (2002). Know-how and workplace practical judgment. *Journal of Philosophy of Education, 34*(2), 281–296.

O'Sullivan, T. (2005). Some theoretical propositions on the nature of practice wisdom. *Journal of Social Work, 5*(2), 221–242.

Ryle, G. (1949). *The concept of mind*. London: Hutchinson.

Schön, D. (1983). *The reflective practitioner: How professionals think in action*. New York: Basic Books.

Schultz, M. (1994). *On studying organizational cultures: Diagnosis and understanding*. New York: Walter de Gruyter.

Sennett, R. (2008). *The craftsman*. New Haven, CT: Yale University Press.

Shaffer, V. A., & Shaffer, L. S. (2006). The use of recipe knowledge in medicine. *International Journal of Technology, Knowledge and Society, 2*(7), 73–80.

Sheppard, M. (1995). Social work, social science and practice wisdom. *British Journal of Social Work, 25*(3), 265–293.

Stevahn, L., King, J. A., Ghere, G., & Minnema, J. (2005). Establishing essential competencies for program evaluators. *American Journal of Evaluation, 26*(1), 43–59.

Wenger, E. (1998). *Communities of practice: Learning, meaning, and identity*. Cambridge, England: Cambridge University Press.

MICHAEL BAIZERMAN *is professor, Youth Studies, School of Social Work, University of Minnesota.*

DONALD W. COMPTON *is former director of evaluation services, National Home Office, American Cancer Society, and adjunct faculty, Emory University, Rollins School of Public Health. He is the corresponding editor for this issue and is reachable at donaldcompton03@comcast.net.*

Baizerman, M. (2009). Deepening understanding of managing evaluation. In D. W. Compton
& M. Baizerman (Eds.), *Managing program evaluation: Towards explicating a professional
practice. New Directions for Evaluation, 121*, 87–98.

8

Deepening Understanding of Managing Evaluation

Michael Baizerman

Abstract

Depth, resonance, and shadow are added to how the expertise of managing evaluation could be grasped and understood. Returning to the notion of "competency" (Stevahn, King, Ghere, & Minnema, 2005), this is contrasted more deeply with Dreyfus and Dreyfus's (2004) conception of expert and to its use in nursing by Benner (2004; Benner, Tanner, & Chelsa, 1996). Dreyfus's five-stage developmental model is presented, as is a sixth stage often not discussed, "practice wisdom" or phronesis, what Strasser (1985) calls "practical science." This notion is explored and its sources in Ancient Greece cited. A beginning exploration is made of lived managing, as is the notion of the "already known." Evaluators are "knowledge workers" (Davenport, 2005), and managing them is central to the work of managing studies and managing an evaluation unit. © Wiley Periodicals, Inc.

I n this chapter, we work to deepen an understanding of managing evaluation as a professional practice, and in this way enrich debate about whether and how to prepare practitioners for competent managing of studies, evaluators, and an evaluation unit. We begin with another elevator trip from the 20th floor to the subbasement, suggesting that one's view and understanding of managing changes dramatically as one ascends and descends. One focus that

changes immediately is a shift from management (20th floor) to managing (ground floor). On the floor of everyday life, managing is a form of expertise.

Expertise as such is the subject of a large literature (Ericsson, Charness, Feltovich, & Hoffman, 2006) and is a frame for understanding managing that complements the model (Stevahn et al., 2005) that uses the language of "competency," with associated knowledge, skills, and dispositions (p. 48). Expertise is oriented to an active praxis wherein knowledge, skills, activities, and context are joined in situations. Expertise in this sense is an active integration of knowledge, activities, skills and moment that together are necessary to do the job that has to be done at high levels of quality and consistency. Examining a well-regarded conception of expertise, we use this to reexamine some elements of the case studies to get at what expertise looks like, how it works, and how it is learned and mastered. This has clear implications for managing. An additional perspective on expertise is found in what we call a "managing gaze."

Managing evaluation is organization work, whether it is managing of studies, workers, or an evaluation unit. We first remember this reality. We then suggest that it is typical to think in modern terms when considering evaluation research and the organizational home of the evaluators, the evaluation unit, and the activity being evaluated. Yet all of these should be thought of both in modern and postmodern terms, as in postmodern evaluation research (Mabry, 1997) done by workers in a postmodern employing agency about programs in an organization that can be a classical modern formal organization or an (emergent) postmodern one (Calas & Smircich, 1999). Interorganizational forms complicate the picture, as, for example, partnerships, coalitions, structures with rhizomic shapes, and the like. All of this complicates effective managing of evaluation, bringing new perspectives, roles, and expertise to the day-to-day work. Among these are new forms of politics, which we briefly explore.

The case studies tell us about organizational hosts of evaluation work, and that evaluation units can be homogeneous (evaluators only) or heterogeneous (evaluators and other scientists or researchers, such as epidemiologists, economists, or sociologists). Managing differs by type of workers, and again (and always) by whether the manager is a trained evaluator. These and similar issues enrich and complicate the basic choice for the evaluation field of whether and how to prepare for competent evaluation managing.

We return to the topic of expertise from another direction. How might we go about learning the core and peripheral situated expertise of managing evaluation? More broadly, what type of practice do we want managing to be? In contrast to models of evidence-based practice developed through applied science, we remind the reader of another type of science, a "practical science" (Strasser, 1985), *phronesis.* We very briefly explore this early Greek notion, along with the basic elements *techné* and *episteme,* and suggest that this type of science and practical wisdom is a good fit for an alternate conception of management science, as Bishop and Scudder (1990) have shown for nursing. Phronesis offers evaluation, a second strategy for developing managing as a scientific, artful, and craftlike practice.

Managerial Skill: Novice to Expert . . . to Practical Science and Practical Wisdom

Stevahn, King, Ghere, and Minnema (2005) clarify and establish essential competencies for program evaluators. The authors review the term *competencies* and its various definitions and uses in building occupational taxonomies. They "choose to use a competency framework that includes knowledge, skills, and dispositions program evaluators need to be effective as professionals." They "choose to write the competencies in behavioral language" (p. 48). "As such, the competencies predominantly describe various activities that evaluators carry out to achieve standards that constitute sound evaluations . . . " (p. 48).

For our purpose, *project management* section (4.0) in Stevahn, King, Ghere, and Minnema is most relevant and includes 12 items (2005, pp. 49–51):

1. Responds to requests for proposals
2. Negotiates with clients before the evaluation begins
3. Writes formal agreements
4. Communicates with clients throughout the evaluation process
5. Budgets an evaluation
6. Justifies cost given information needs
7. Identifies needed resources for evaluation, such as information, expertise, personnel, instruments
8. Uses appropriate technology
9. Supervises others involved in conducting the evaluation
10. Trains others involved in conducting the evaluation
11. Conducts the evaluation nondisruptively
12. Presents work in a timely manner

Competency is correlated to task and activity and can be trained; expert(ise) is earned in prolonged practice. In contrast, much of what is crucial to managing evaluators as knowledge workers, as researchers, as professionals, is not easily trained, and the same is true for managing a unit.

In contrast to Stevahn et al. (2005), the approach here is to attend to the expertise of managing evaluation. For that purpose, the work of Dreyfus and Dreyfus (2004) is well suited. In their several papers (1988, 2004, 2005) and the adaptation of their work to nursing (Benner, 2004; Benner, et al., 1996; Benner, Hooper-Kyriakidis, & Stannard, 1999), they lay out a five-level model of skill acquisition and performance emphasizing how mastery works in everyday practice, how at the expert level phronesis, practical wisdom, or practical science is done by a trained and experienced practitioner. In nursing, the moment is critical, often at the edge of life and death, and the practitioner must act at once and be right (and good) in her thought-action. This action in the tense and critical moment is crucial for our work because, life and death aside, most managers, and surely those at high levels in public agencies, work in frenetic, active, relentless spaces where information, tasks, and decision needs come toward them all the time, and where these are experienced as bursts of demands, information, and needs coming at them from all directions, endlessly.

Dreyfus (2001) presents the Dreyfus and Dreyfus five-stage skill acquisition model:

1. Novice
2. Advanced beginner
3. Competence
4. Proficiency
5. Expertise

Paraphrased, each stage of "skill acquisition" can be characterized in these ways.

Stage One: Novice. The primary work of the beginner is to recognize general or noncontextual features of the work, the "task environment," and to learn whether, when, and how to act on the basis of these features. The novice needs facts and context for making sense. The beginning manager is rule-based. Some examples for evaluation managing:

• Here are guidelines for the 14 steps necessary to complete a contract for an evaluation study by an external contractor. Parameters for each step are given, as are a set of proscribed actions. Preferred actions are also presented.
• This is a set of rules for how to avoid conflict with supervisors.
• A good manager will ensure that every meeting has a printed and distributed agenda.

Stage Two: Advanced Beginner. The novice manager dealing with real situations begins to learn about relevant context for understanding, decision, and action. She gets better at picking up on what is general and what is situational. The advanced beginner manager now uses maxims. Some examples for evaluation managing:

• Talk with employees about racial tensions in the evaluation unit directly, clearly, and objectively. Should you always do this? When should you not do this? Under what conditions?
• Let your evaluators know that you have 17 years of experience in designing and implementing evaluation studies in schools. Should you say this when supervising epidemiologists in a health department evaluation group? Why so, and why not?

- How do you go about negotiating study cost at an agency with little, some, or a lot of money for such studies? Does a similar study cost the same for whoever wants it?
- When is it wrong to. . . .

Stage Three: Competence. The beginning manager now practically and accurately uses what she learned on real-world examples and in her work world. She now has her own orientation, perspective, and plan about whether and how to do the work, while also wondering if she has got it right. Here are some examples for evaluation managing:

- We got to the agency and there were no records there.
- One evaluator said that another evaluator was "cooking the data."
- The manager has only a B.A., while the evaluators she supervises all have Ph.D.s.
- The lead evaluator is pregnant and having medical problems and can't be available to present study rationale and progress to the agency board.

Stage Four: Proficiency. Movement to proficiency requires moving from grasping and understanding information to becoming involved in actual situations. Now, experience and information are brought together and assimilated. The manager is able to make situational determinations. She has intuitive responses, simply seeing what needs to be done. She "gets it" rather than calculates. Then the manager must act, and to get there she must decide whether and how. She now uses the earlier rules and maxims. The manager at this level sees what has to be done and has to "figure out" whether and how to do it. Some examples for evaluation managing:

- Let's cancel the research contract because people who would miss three meetings just don't follow through on other tasks.
- I'm sure that another meeting with the staff as a whole would be effective in diminishing confusion over this policy.
- Go talk to Maria; she knows how it works.

Stage Five: Expertise. Expertise in managing evaluation is shown when the worker sees both what needs to be done and how to do it well (and good). Using her "vast repertoire of situational discriminations," "what must be done simply is done" (Dreyfus, 2001, p. 42). As Aristotle put it, the expert "straightaway" does what is appropriate. Some examples for evaluation managing:

- Go talk to Maria; use my name. She gets it, has access, and can make it work.
- Cancel the contract because it isn't working, and we have a lot of other work to do.
- Let's have another staff meeting because the group is ready to work it out.

Dreyfus (2001) goes beyond these five stages, adding "mastery" as the highest level of skill, and also adds a seventh stage: "practical wisdom" (p. 46). This is the classical Greek phronesis (Bishop & Scudder, 1990; Dunne, 1993; Strasser, 1985), "the general ability to do the appropriate thing, at the appropriate time, in the appropriate way." To Strasser (1985), this can be practical science, while to others it is "practice wisdom."

Managing as Phronesis

This stage model of expertise is a useful conception of the expertise of managing evaluation, with implications for education and training. Managing is most invisible when the subject is research.

Managing evaluation studies is an almost universal practice. Yet it is difficult for some to distinguish it from implementing a study. This became clear to us in an editor's response to a paper we submitted on managing evaluation studies. We wrote about managing evaluation studies as invisible practice, as we do here. She said that what we were examining is good evaluation design, feasibility, and accuracy. Her electronic search turned up almost 1,000 hits for *program evaluation,* and she suggested that we go back to the literature and in effect start over. This issue is one response to her invitation.

In the case studies, it is hard to focus on managing a single study because "there is so much going on" that one study is quiet work, only a small part of the unit's work, typically not laced with tension or conflict for the unit as a whole and quite routine; this is everyday work for many evaluators working in evaluation groups or on their own. Managing is more easily seen *as managing* when examined in the context of multiple studies. In our perspective, getting a study done and used requires managing the study.

Two questions make a visible and crucial distinction between managing and implementing one or more evaluation studies:

- What is the best science for this study?
- What is the best way to make this science happen?

These simple questions make explicit the reality that every evaluation study results from a set of evaluator decisions about "how best to," that is, the best science to design and implement (and use) the study right now, under these conditions. This is at minimum about "evaluability," and more inclusively about a study in this context with these resources, now. Also made explicit here is that these technical evaluation decisions, after being made, have to be made real in the world of a program and organization. Managing one or more evaluation studies is this making real. It is easier to see this when we move from managing a single evaluation study to managing a set of studies, a group of evaluators and other workers, or an evaluation unit.

We have distinguished managing from implementing an evaluation study. Next we go in another direction, away from classical evaluation studies and away from classical organizational forms, from the modern to the postmodern.

Modern and Postmodern Evaluation in and of Modern and Postmodern Organizations: Managing New Evaluation Approaches in New Contexts

Almost all the literature on evaluation studies is modernist in its philosophical assumptions, strategies, methods, and practices. There is one text—Mabry (1997)—introducing postmodern evaluation, with its "relentless quandaries regarding reality, textual and political representation, methodology, culture for evaluating quality, authority and roles, ethics, values and responsibilities" (p. 10). Mabry opens a dialogue with modernist conceptions about what is evaluation and how to go about it. Postmodernism interrogates the very assumptions and ways of typical evaluation work. There is an older and much larger postmodernist literature in organization theory and research (Boje, Gephart, & Thatchenkery, 1996). Basic to this work is a reconceptualizing of organizations away from hierarchical bureaucratic forms to networks, formal intersystems, with rhizomic and other shapes. Postmodern management also has a literature (Boje et al., 1996) with an emphasis on the managing of these new organizational forms, typically in real environments in which managerial control is limited, horizontal, and emergent.

For our purpose, it is important to consider possible consequences of these perspectives, scholarship, and everyday realities on managing evaluation studies, workers, and an evaluation unit. With postmodernism presenting a challenge to the consensus on the right or best way to do the science of a study, what must the manager of evaluation studies know, if anything, about these debates and their implications for the technical choices and details of studies? This is a basic question throughout this issue. The question takes on another hue when professional disagreements within a modernist frame are challenged by those (postmodernists) who problematize the frame itself. Managing the evaluator as a postmodern knowledge worker in a postmodern organization is a more complex process than managing a modernist evaluator in a modernist organization. Managing an evaluation unit of postmodern knowledge workers in a postmodern organization that is networklike or rhizomic in structure is also more complex.

Everyday Managing and Everyday Politics: The Elephant in the Sandbox

Whether modern or postmodern, whether the organization is public or private, there is politics. Given several individuals, several organizational units, and several projects, there will be "politics"—the ongoing negotiation over purpose, authority, power, projects, product, and prestige. This is basic to managing and is omnipresent in organization work.

In some organizations at middle-management positions, politics is a reality that is lived, spoken, and unwritten. Managing is written about as if politics were not always there, not braided into life. Politics is airbrushed out of the picture and out of managing accounts.

In contrast, politics is taken for granted here and conceived of as co-present in every aspect of managing. Managing is in a sense political—political action, from initiating requests to formulating studies to implementing them, and then using them for policy, program improvement, and the rest. In a post-modern sense, (almost) everything in managing is woven through the politics of interpretation (hermeneutics), meaning, representation, and action. There is no expertise in managing evaluation that is not braided with the political.

Managing as a political process is in part the managing of time and work, of moments, situations, events, and the flows of people, activities, and all the rest. Earlier essays have focused on the organizational-structural in the manager's position. Next we move from the manager's structural location to what it is like to be in that location—the lived-experience of being a manager gets us closer to lived managing.

What Is Evaluation Managing? Toward Lived-Practice

The case studies in our earlier elevator metaphor (Chapter 1) are at the 10th to fifth floors, with occasional stops on the ground floor. In this section, we move between the fifth floor (some abstraction and conceptualization) to the ground floor (and below)—everyday practice as told, described, and lived—that is, managing as lived practice. This is the level of what it is like to do managing and to be a manager (and *to be* one's managing). This is the level of expertise as *lived experience*. This level is crucial to the more advanced stages of skill acquisition in the Dreyfus model (2001) as such, and in how Benner, Tanner, and Chelsa use it in nursing (1996).

The manager managing is located in constant flows of moments, situations and events—life-flows. Managing is working in the midst of these flows as they become moments and these become activities, decisions, meetings, tasks, and other recognizable shapes of everyday life at work. In the "natural attitude" (Berger & Luckmann, 1966) of mundane taken-for-granted work, the world presents itself to the manager managing as "stuff" to pay attention to, or as stuff to notice and let pass. One pays attention to what one needs for one's purpose-at-hand, here and now or for some larger, longer-term purpose, such as next year's project proposal or evaluation capacity building (Compton, Baizerman, & Stockdill, 2002).

The manager is embedded in an organization, and that structural position locates him in multiple flows, some more likely to come, some more regular, some more appropriate. What will and does come the way of the manager always depends in part on his organizational position mediated by the manager's work projects and other elements in his work field. Organizational structure and individual consciousness both regulate work flow, and in this way they serve to create what (managing) needs to be done, when, and to some extent how. Managing to the manager is about everyday work flow within larger time frames.

Managing Workers: Evaluators and Other Employees

The manager manages workers, whether in homogeneous (all professional evaluators) or heterogeneous evaluation groups. Whether called and perceived as evaluators, scientists, knowledge workers (Davenport, 2005), or simply as workers or staff, most managers in almost every organization must manage employees. Is there anything unique to managing evaluation research, whether or not in a named evaluation unit with responsibility for evaluation research? Using the case studies, the literature and our experience (and others'), we think not. What uniqueness is seen lies in evaluation as such, this particular science and craft, and whether the manager and the workers come from and belong to the evaluation community of practice. As we show in Chapter 9, there are several possible combinations of evaluation membership by manager and workers. Each requires a somewhat different managing expertise. That is how it always is for managers and workers from the same or differing professional fields. All differences that count lie in the particulars. What is important is to recognize evaluators as "knowledge workers" (Davenport, 2005).

Treating evaluators as knowledge workers allows us to use that literature to illuminate the managing of evaluators, other researchers, and other employees in the evaluation unit. The basic idea in this literature is that today's professionals "have a high degree of expertise, education, or experience, and the primary purpose of their jobs involves the creation, distribution, or application of knowledge" (Davenport, 2005, p. 10). Effectively managing knowledge workers may require a shift in the manager's orientation. This might include a change from overseeing work to joining in doing it, from supporting the bureaucracy to fending it off, and from organizing hierarchies of workers to organizing communities of workers.

In practical, everyday terms, there are a variety of everyday, mundane issues specific to this class of employee, some of which place the manager between organizational policies and his efforts to maximize the knowledge workers' productivity and commitment to the organization. For example:

- How much flexibility in work schedule and time working out of the office should be allowed?
- How can the knowledge worker's need for autonomy best be addressed?
- How can the worker's contribution best be measured by the organization's performance evaluation system and reward structure?

NEW DIRECTIONS FOR EVALUATION • DOI: 10.1002/ev

- How can professional and personal development best be supported?
- What kind of work environment is most conducive to enhancing worker performance and results?

Managing evaluators is like managing other knowledge workers from one's own profession or another, or community of practice, except in the particulars, and there do not seem to be many issues in evaluation not found in managing other research. We do not give much space here to this most important aspect of day-to-day managing. To remind, it is our purpose to make visible managing as everyday practice, and to use this visibility and understanding of managing to answer broad questions about whether the evaluation profession should recognize managing as a core expertise, and support education and training in this. Differences specific to evaluation can be drawn from studies and anecdotes of actual practice.

Lurking behind and below this and all the other topics in this issue are the larger, more encompassing, and complex themes of what expertise is, how it shows itself and how it works, and what types of expertise constitute "managing evaluation." These themes sit on even more general issues about knowledge as such and its different types and forms (epistemology). We enter this thicket of foundational thought at its edge and then move in only a few inches to propose a classical conception of knowledge that fits well our exploration of managing evaluation as practical expertise.

What Type of Knowledge Is Managing Expertise?

There is a long-term debate about what a manager must know about and know how to do. Some argue for management science as the core, others for organization science or evaluation science. Managing as a practice can be joined to them or be seen as itself a core science. In this view it is an applied science. Another historical strand can be used to understand managing differently, as a practical science (Strasser, 1985), the Greek phronesis.

Current science-based disciplines and professions typically are in the language world and epistemologies of episteme or techné, science or craft. Medical, engineering, and management science are in the world of techné— the world of practical affairs, of practical, everyday professions, events, acts, and actions. Phronesis, practical science or practical wisdom, is another conception of science, one oriented to how to work in specific situations, doing what is technically right (correct), and for some authors joining this to what is normatively and morally good. We name a distinction between managing as an applied science in the frame of management science (episteme and techné) and managing as a practical science (phronesis). This is a distinction with a difference. In relocating managing to the frame of phronesis, a new strategy is available for building and using this practical science. In effect, managing can be thought of as embodied and lived practice, not only the application of (objective) knowledge.

The Already Know(n)

What we are trying to get at with the words "already known" is a form of knowledge that is integrated in expertise and comes, typically in the case of professionals, from extended study and long work experience. It may be thought of as a type of "recipe knowledge" (Berger and Luckmann, 1966), "knowledge limited to programmatic competence in routine performances." This knowledge is also a type of practice wisdom (O'Sullivan, 2005). It can be heard in phrases such as these: "Been there, done that"; "Here we go again"; "Same old, same old"; "That again?!" More formally, "If things are thus, I can act as I have already acted." It is commonsense knowledge within a community of practice's "stock of knowledge" wherein expertise is defined and flourishes (Berger & Luckmann, 1966).

The already known is more than experience; it is found as an essential of expertise. It is part of the answer to the question posed by Collins and Evans (2007): What does it mean "to know what you are talking about" (p. 2)? It is neither cookbook knowledge nor recipe knowledge in the limited everyday sense. It is more the repertoire of connoisseurship and discernment.

References

Benner, P. (2004). Using the Dreyfus model of skill acquisition to describe and interpret skill acquisition and clinical judgment in nursing practice and education. *Bulletin of Science, Technology & Society, 24*(3), 188–199.

Benner, P., Hooper-Kyriakidis, P., & Stannard, D. (1999). *Clinical wisdom and interventions in critical care: A thinking-in-action approach.* Philadelphia: Saunders.

Benner, P., Tanner, C. A., & Chelsa, C. A. (1996). *Expertise in nursing practice: Caring, clinical judgment and ethics.* New York: Springer.

Berger, P., & Luckmann, T. (1966). *The social construction of reality: A treatise in the sociology of knowledge.* New York: Anchor Books, Doubleday.

Bishop, A. H., & Scudder, J. R. (1990). *The practical, moral, and personal sense of nursing: A phenomenological philosophy of practice.* Albany: State University of New York Press.

Boje, D. M., Gephart, R. P., & Thatchenkery, T. J. (Eds.). (1996). *Postmodern management and organization theory.* Thousand Oaks, CA: Sage.

Calas, M. B., & Smircich, L. (1999). Past postmodernism? Reflections and tentative directions. *Academy of Management Review, 24*(4), 649–671.

Collins, H., & Evans, R. (2007). *Rethinking expertise.* Chicago: University of Chicago Press.

Compton, D., Baizerman, M., & Stockdill, S. (Eds.). (2002). *The art, craft, and science of evaluation capacity building. New Directions for Evaluation, 93,* 1–120.

Davenport, T. H. (2005). *Thinking for a living: How to get better performance and results from knowledge workers.* Boston: Harvard Business School Press.

Dreyfus, H. (2001). *On the Internet (thinking in action).* New York: Routledge.

Dreyfus, H. L., & Dreyfus, S. E. (1988). *Mind over machine.* New York: Free Press.

Dreyfus, H. L., & Dreyfus, S. E. (2004). The ethical implications of five-stage skill acquisition model. *Bulletin of Science, Technology, and Society, 24*(3), 251–264.

Dreyfus, H. L., & Dreyfus, S. E. (2005). Peripheral vision: Expertise in real world contexts. *Organization Studies, 26*(5), 779–792.

Dunne, J. (1993). *Back to the rough ground: "Phronesis" and "techne" in modern philosophy and in Aristotle.* Notre Dame, IN: University of Notre Dame Press.

Ericsson, K. A., Charness, N., Feltovich, P. J., & Hoffman, R. R. (Eds.). (2006). *The Cambridge handbook of expertise and expert performance*. Cambridge, England: Cambridge University Press.

Mabry, L. (1997). *Advances in program evaluation: Evaluation and the postmodern dilemma*. Greenwich, CT: JAI Press.

O'Sullivan, T. (2005). Some theoretical propositions on the nature of practice wisdom. *Journal of Social Work, 5*(2), 221–242.

Stevahn, L., King, J. A., Ghere, G., & Minnema, J. (2005). Establishing essential competencies for program evaluators. *American Journal of Evaluation, 26*(1), 43–59.

Strasser, S. (1985). *Understanding and explanation: Basic ideas concerning the humanity of the human sciences*. Pittsburgh: Duquesne University Press.

MICHAEL BAIZERMAN *is professor, youth studies, School of Social Work, University of Minnesota.*

Baizerman, M., & Compton, D. W. (2009). Toward developing competent evaluation managing. In D. W. Compton & M. Baizerman (Eds.), *Managing program evaluation: Towards explicating a professional practice. New Directions for Evaluation, 121*, 99–109.

9

Toward Developing Competent Evaluation Managing

Michael Baizerman, Donald W. Compton

Abstract

Here the essentials of the expertise of managing are presented as orientation toward (ethos, stance, and gaze), knowledge about, and knowledge how-to ("know-how"). These are grounded to specific content, summarized, and then connected to a typology of managing evaluation. The orienting questions for the field are reviewed to reveal what it means to prepare expert evaluation managers and expertise in managing evaluation. This includes very brief introductions to curricula, pedagogy, and learning styles. A short discussion presents a proposed managing career path for evaluators and nonevaluators. The chapter ends with two answers to focal questions of the text and a stance for the profession on the practice and preparation for managing evaluation. © Wiley Periodicals, Inc.

> Your unit heads may think that managing talented producers and performers raises special problems, but I been in sugar all my life and I can assure you that the management of people in television is *precisely the same as management* of sugar workers.
>
> —(Quoted in Collins & Evans, 2007, p. 5; emphasis ours)

H ere we present and examine briefly what we think is basic and necessary for deciding as a field if we want to develop managing expertise, and if so, the necessary elements of education and training. We
begin with a general orientation to managing evaluation, including ethos,
stance, gaze, and knowledge, and specify these for managing studies, evaluators and other workers, and an evaluation unit.

What Must an Evaluation Manager Know?

Our purpose here is to begin a conversation with the field on the expertise
in managing evaluation. In what follows we have used the companion chapters in this issue of *NDE* and the specific literature on managing social science, health, and education research, along with our own practice (Tarling,
2006; Bush and Bell, 2002).

Expertise incorporates ethos, stance, and gaze (Compton, Baizerman, &
Stockdill, 2002), and these are joined to knowledge and skill, knowledge
about and knowledge how to (Ryle, 1949). A gaze is a way of noticing, seeing, interpreting, and understanding. There is position gaze, the ways of
noticing linked directly to an organizational structural location. Gaze is also
part of core professional perception and of each individual's personal way
of seeing. What are the elements of a general orientation to managing evaluation? See Table 9.1.

This general orientation to managing evaluation includes ethos, stance,
and gaze. Expertise is more than these; it is also knowledge and skill. Using
Ryle's distinction (1949), here is proposed minimum knowledge in managing evaluation for reflection and debate within our field (Table 9.2).

Expertise lies in embodying this knowledge and doing and reflecting
on it consistently and at a high degree of effectiveness, as defined by a particular community of practice—in this case, those who are expert in managing studies, workers, or evaluation units (Wenger, 1998). Expertise in
managing—high-level know-how—is contextual and situational, depend-
ing on employing an organization's structure, culture, processes and practices, and the like (Alvesson, 1993; Schultz, 1994). In the case of managing
evaluation, a crucial factor is the manager's professional education and training. Using this factor, we next present a typology of managing evaluation
and join to it the general orientation and minimum knowledge for evaluation managers.

A Typology of Managing Evaluation

Using the manager's professional background and knowledge about how to
do professional evaluation research as the key factors, we present six types
of arrangement. These were taken from the case studies, interviews, the literature, and our long professional experience. Left out is skill because it is
context- and situation-dependent; managing evaluators and other workers

Table 9.1. Orientation, Knowledge, and Expertise in Effective Managing of Evaluation

Elements of a General Orientation to Managing Evaluation		Core Knowledge Domains
Ethos	• Evaluation science is a legitimate type of social research • Evaluation science is a professional practice guided by AEA standards • Evaluation science is a practical science (phronesis) • Evaluation science is used to learn about effectiveness in the context of accountability, program improvement, ECB, and the like • There is an identifiable evaluation expertise orientation recognizable as thinking and perceiving and acting "evaluatively" • Programmatic interventions can be understood and possibly improved using evaluation	Managing as such	• General conceptions and theories of management, manager role, and managing • Basic, general managerial roles and responsibilities • Managing as organizational practice • Project management of grants and contracts • Evaluation-specific ethos, stance, gaze, and technical knowledge about evaluation research approaches and methods
Stance	• Evaluation managers facilitate the evaluation enterprise and evaluation studies • Evaluators work from identifiable and legitimate bodies of scholarly and professional knowledge • Evaluation managers work to ensure that evaluators and the evaluation unit do quality, ethical professional studies using The Program Evaluation Standards (Joint Committee on Standards for Educational Evaluation, 1994) • Evaluations must meet client wants and needs as mutually agreed • Evaluation studies are done to be used	Organizations	• Organization as the primary work context, environment, and field of play • Models of organizational types, e.g., formal and nonformal, public and private; NGO (nongovernmental) and CBO (community-based), etc. • General theories about organizations (e.g., structure, size, age, interorganizational structures [networks, coalitions], culture, relations, rules, procedures, etc.), modern and postmodern • Specific models of evaluation research organizations and units
Gaze	• Professional evaluators perceive and imagine the possibilities of evaluation studies of interventions and the contributions possible to enhance the effectiveness and efficiency of these interventions	Evaluation	See Table 9.2

Table 9.2. Toward Minimum Required Knowledge in Managing Evaluation

About	How To
Proposed Minimum Required Knowledge About Evaluation As Such • Evaluation is a professional field distinct from research • Evaluation is a legitimate practical and applied science • The general purpose of evaluation is as a social practice • Evaluation has real consequences • Evaluation research uses a variety of strategies and methods depending on the situation and contract • Evaluation science has similarities to and differences from other social and behavioral sciences	**Proposed Minimum Required Knowledge on How to Do Evaluation Research** • Knows "systematic inquiry" in evaluation research (Stevahn, King, Ghere, and Minnema, 2005) • Thinks evaluatively; in that mind-set • Can contribute to the development of evaluation staff on evaluation research approaches and methods • Knows Joint Standards for Evaluation/AEA Guidelines
Minimum Knowledge About Evaluators • May have explicit, focused, and sustained preparation as evaluator in one or more disciplines or professions • How evaluators think evaluatively; in this mind-set • Have professional identity as an evaluator • May belong to and participate in a professional group of or on evaluation (e.g., AEA) • Evaluators' systematic inquiry in ways recognizable as evaluation by professionally trained and practicing evaluators (community of practice)	**Minimum Knowledge on How to Work with Evaluators** • Must accept evaluation science as a legitimate science of the social • Must accept evaluators practicing evaluation research as legitimate and equal scientific colleagues • Must include evaluation professionals in policy making and other discussions that affect their professional role as evaluators • Must seek evaluator input on design, implementation, and use of studies
Minimum Knowledge About an Evaluation Unit • When the unit is an evaluation unit, its primary purpose is doing practical and usable evaluation research • Evaluation units can be homogeneous (only evaluators) or heterogeneous (evaluation scientists and other scientists) • Trained, professional evaluators have major input into designing and implementing evaluation studies and their use • Evaluation units may be politically contested spaces because all evaluation studies have real-world consequences for programs, budget, staff, policies, and the like • Evaluation units may have extensive networks both inside and outside their home organization	**Minimum Knowledge on How to Manage a Unit** • Must be politically savvy and effective working tridirectionally (above, across, below) • Must understand how to sustain and lead the unit in the context of the organization and its environments, including building demand for evaluation and its use • Must be able to understand and facilitate development of the unit's relationship with external partners, funding organizations, and the larger community • Must have working knowledge of the organization's policies, e.g., personnel, budget, contracting

and an evaluation unit are omitted to keep the example from becoming too long and too complex. A classical Weberian ideal-type strategy was used in which one item among several found together in the world is emphasized to show unnoticed or unappreciated relationships (Gerth and Mills, 1946).

Consider the discussions, confusions, tensions, negotiations, and work styles that may characterize everyday life in evaluation units with each particular configuration of manager and evaluators.

Six Arrangements for Managing Evaluation.

1. Manager is expert in managing and expert in evaluation (case studies)
2. Manager is expert in managing and has little or no competence, knowledge, or experience with evaluation
3. Manager is expert in evaluation and has little or no competence, knowledge, or experience in managing as such
4. Manager knows little or nothing about both managing and evaluation
5. Manager knows managing but not evaluation (has staff person who is expert in evaluation)
6. Manager knows evaluation but not managing (has staff person who is expert manager)

Type One: Expert in Managing and Conducting Evaluation Studies. The manager began a professional career as a professionally trained evaluator who was promoted to manager after years of demonstrating enthusiasm for and competence in completing evaluation studies. He was formally trained and formally and informally mentored in managing studies, colleagues and, later, an evaluation unit. He sees himself as a competent evaluator and manager, and is seen in these ways by colleagues he manages and by those who supervise him. He is the consummate pro, noticeably adept at working the system for his unit and staff and their evaluation work.

Here the manager shares ethos, stance, and gaze with evaluation colleagues whom he manages, that is, the workers. He also has similar knowledge about evaluation research and how to carry out studies; the manager is like his workers.

The manager also holds and lives a managing ethos, stance, and gaze, and the knowledge to grasp and act managerially with evaluation colleagues.

Type Two: Expert in Managing Only. The manager began a professional career as a management intern after graduating in "management." She is doing what she has always wanted to do, which is helping others do their work. She and others see her competence in planning, budgeting, personnel, and representing the unit in the larger organization. She is an effective protector of and advocate for staff but does not have a good grasp of what they actually do, though understanding the general purpose of their evaluation work and some of the realities they face implementing studies. She could see herself managing in a school, a hospital, or a fire department and is clear about management orientation and competence and the limits of her knowledge about the context the staff is working on. She manages knowledge workers and an organizational unit that happens to be working on evaluation research.

Here the manager holds a managing ethos, stance, and gaze, and the necessary knowledge about and how to manage but does not hold any of these for evaluation research. The manager understands the job as facilitating and supporting evaluators in their research. This manager may or may not like to work with evaluators and sees herself as expert in managing, which could be done in other settings. Professional identity is as manager. The manager may have little in common with workers' professional interests or professional identity.

Type Three: Expert in Evaluation Only. The manager began his professional career as a professionally trained evaluator who was promoted to manager after years demonstrating his enthusiasm for and competence in completing evaluation studies. His calling, love, and identity are as an evaluator. He sees himself and is seen by others as a "loner" who prefers to work alone or with other evaluation researchers, and he shows little interest and competence in managing other people or their research. He dislikes doing personnel reviews and constructing budgets and finds meetings with other managers as time away from research and therefore wasted. He would happily return to full-time research with no managerial responsibilities, but he is the senior researcher, and no one else in the unit has his knowledge, experience, and reputation.

The manager here shares ethos, stance, gaze, and knowledge about evaluation research with evaluators in the unit being managed. He does not share any of these with other managers in his organization; nor is he a master of managing. Professional identity may be as an evaluator, but surely it is not as a manager.

Type Four: Manager Knows Little About Managing or Evaluation. The manager came to be in this position because he passed exams that led to promotions, and then to a promotion to an organizational position called manager. It first happened to be in a unit doing evaluation research. His primary orientation is to do his best for his employing organization, and he does this by doing what he is asked and told to do: budget, plan, manage personnel, work on task groups with other managers, and the like. To himself, he is an employee, an executive, neither a manager nor an evaluator, and to himself and others he is competent in neither. He does the job without a deep grasp of the unit's purpose, practices, and meanings. Sometimes a manager gets the position in a reorganization, having lost his position. He was placed in this position because he was available, someone with experience in the organization who was needed or wanted, and he is known.

This manager holds the professional identity of neither an evaluator nor a manager and knows little about the work of the workers or of a manager.

Type Five: Manager Knows Managing and Has Staff Expert in Evaluation. Aware of her domain of knowledge, competence, and experience and of her limited grasp of evaluation, the manager has a close associate she supervises who is expert in evaluation research. This person serves as her agent and advocate on technical issues in evaluation research, as well as on the broader understanding of the evaluation enterprise and its social, cultural, political, and economic aspects, and as a sociocultural agent and interpreter.

Aware of her own managing expertise and own lack of knowledge about the evaluation enterprise, she has someone who, in effect and in practice, manages the evaluators as evaluators and the evaluations, while the manager focuses on administrative duties and defers to the assistant for technical and content-related decisions.

Type Six: Manager Knows Evaluation and Has Staff Expert Manager. Aware of her domain expertise in evaluation research, but neither in managing colleagues nor a unit, the manager has a staff person who manages, that is, does personnel, budget, planning, and other necessary and regular managerial and administrative work. The manager is the titular head of the unit, but in effect her expert manager manages the unit, except for the research studies and the evaluators as evaluators; as employees, her agent is their boss, while as evaluators she is their colleague, supervisor, manager, and boss.

In this arrangement, the manager works primarily with evaluators and their research, turning over the management of the unit to an expert manager who does not have a professional identity or expertise in evaluation.

In this typology, each of the six types of manager arrangements is likely to show its own evaluation unit work culture and tone, with different configurations of work styles, worker-manager communications, (mis)understandings, and the like. These were presented heuristically to suggest that the expertise—the general orientation (ethos, stance, gaze), minimal knowledge (about and how), and skill—of managing evaluation is highly context-dependent. So it is also in all professions. (For an excellent insight into nursing, see Benner, et al., 1996.)

This means that preparation of managers expert in managing evaluation has to be grounded in context and situation, as well as in principles, values, and knowledge. Managing is a complex praxis of all of this, including ethos, stance, gaze, knowledge, and skill put into practical use correctly and rightly for the situation at hand.

This implies that expertise in managing can be learned, and to do so requires curricula, pedagogy, and learning sites—some of which must be in the everyday world of evaluation managing, as Dreyfus (2001) makes clear.

Preparing Expert Managers and Developing Managing Expertise

Curricula. There are few existing curricula specific to managing evaluation. Bell (2004) writes about managing evaluation projects and has offered a workshop, Management for Evaluators and Those with Oversight Responsibility, at the Evaluator's Institute, with short-term professional development courses for practicing evaluators (see www.evaluatorsinstitute.com). He addresses six areas of evaluation management: selecting the evaluator(s), developing rational work plans, organizing staff for results, making assignments productive, monitoring interim progress, and ensuring product quality and usefulness. The vast literature on management and the evaluation literature also contain resources for developing curricula (Lunt, Davidson, & McKegg, 2003; Owen, 2007; Western Michigan University Checklist project, www.wmich.edu/evalctr/checklists/).

Curricula must fit with pedagogy and learning sites, as Dewey, Montrosse, Schröter, and Sullins (2008) note for evaluation. Ideal in our view would be curricula co-created by working evaluation managers, university faculty and students, and practicing evaluators. A goal would be curricula adaptable to several families of education, pedagogy, and learning sites.

Curricula would be oriented to developing managing experience in evaluation and the two forms of knowledge and practical skill in managing. The goal would be producing expertise in managing evaluation studies, workers, and an evaluation unit.

Pedagogy. There are families of education and training pedagogies for learning knowledge about and knowledge how-to. In professional practice and learning, knowledge is joined to values and to a moral base (Benner, 1994).

It is not possible to prepare experts during a single moment; it takes time and movement from less to more knowledge and skill. This is clear in Dreyfus and all other models. In classical forms of Western or Eastern mastery of craft, such as weaving and potting, learning is organized as apprentice to a master who is teacher, mentor, and coach of the rules of thumb, practice wisdom, tacit knowledge, and other types of relevant knowledge—about and how to do the craft and live as this type of craftsperson. In craft, one common learning model is learning at the foot of the master, to do and also *to be* a certain type of person, such as a weaver. Ideally, knowledge, values, skills, and personal identity come to be integrated. Where practical (manageable size, reasonable cost, sufficient time), this type of learning can be made a real and practical approach to bringing workers—evaluators and others—into the managing evaluation community of practice.

Sites. A range of sites could be used to teach a core curriculum on managing evaluation. Examples are workshops at the Annual Meeting of the American Evaluation Association, the Evaluator's Institute, the CDC/AEA Summer Institute, and university courses in a range of fields, including education, public health, social work, and psychology.

However, workshop and classroom are insufficient and wrong for higher-level mastery (Dreyfus, 2001). Necessary are experiential learning structures to master the praxis that is expertise, and to master it at the level of phronesis—practical wisdom, what Aristotle called excellence. Dewey et al. (2008) explore similar issues in evaluation as "other training opportunities" (p. 27). On the job learning will be crucial for mastery, and necessary for working professionals.